Mrs John B. Miller
13 Pleasant Pky
Buffalo N.Y.

PICTORIAL HISTORY

OF THE

SECOND WORLD WAR

A PHOTOGRAPHIC RECORD
OF ALL THEATERS OF ACTION
CHRONOLOGICALLY ARRANGED

VOL. 2

New York
WM. H. WISE and CO., INC.
1944

Printed in the United States of America

CONTENTS

ACKNOWLEDGMENTS

Photographs in this publication were obtained from the following sources:

Official U. S. Navy Photographs —Pages 574, 575, 576, 577, 578,
579, 664, 665, 675, 682, 683,
696, 697, 698, 728, 729, 730,
731, 732, 733, 788, 789, 816,
817, 843, 894, 920, 921, 938,
939, 946, 947, 950, 951, 968,
969, 970, 971, 972, 973, 1016

Acme Newspictures, Inc. —Pages 594, 595, 596, 597, 602,
603, 606, 607, 608, 609, 651,
652, 660, 661, 700, 701, 702,
703, 716, 738, 739, 764, 765,
773, 839, 960, 996, 997

U. S. Army Signal Corps Photos —Pages 650, 675, 676, 677, 678,
679, 735, 822, 823, 826, 827,
902, 903, 906, 907, 966, 967

Army Air Forces Photos —Pages 654, 655, 666, 667, 736,
746, 784, 785, 824, 825, 842

Official U. S. Marine Corps Photos—Pages 731, 732, 747, 748, 749,
750, 751, 753, 758, 790, 791,
808, 809, 948, 949

British Combine Photos, Ltd. —Pages 742, 743, 852

Official Coast Guard Photos —Pages 752, 1017, 1018, 1019

All other Odhams Press.

FOREWORD

FOR a number of reasons, the reader may find the second volume of the PICTORIAL HISTORY OF THE SECOND WORLD WAR even more gratifying than the first. These pages depict American participation in the world combat, a factor of significance to those who have relatives in the services. We have taken special care to show American fighting men in action in all the various theaters where their increasing strength began to turn the tide of victory. The excellent photographic corps of the Army, Navy, Marines and Coast Guard have created a comprehensive pictorial bibliography of the events in the Solomons, New Guinea, North Africa and Sicily, places where troops from the United States played decisive roles.

From the purely dramatic point of view, the third and fourth years were frought with climactic battles, upon which the camera did an exceptional reportorial job. We have read much about the treachery of Pearl Harbor. But the pictures of the sunken "Arizona", the limp "California" and the capsized "Oklahoma" under the pall of smoke over Oahu really bring home the monumental nature of the disaster.

From the Russian front we have some great shots of the bloody battle of Stalingrad where the issue was fought from street to street and door to door until the Nazis went down to critical defeat. The naval engagements in the Coral Sea and at Midway Island, where the American Navy crushed Japanese hopes, are superlatively portrayed. In the Mediterranean theater, we are taken from the initial landings at Casablanca and Algiers through the Tunisian campaign to the conquest of Sicily. The minor but sanguinary retaking of Attu and the unresisted reoccupation of Kiska are both recorded.

These are but a few of the action phases we have recorded from the many battlefronts of the second world war. As in volume one, we have introduced each year with a brief running story of the highlights of that period. If this chronology seems sketchy, the onus must be jointly shared by the complexities of global war and our resolve to make these volumes a pictorial history and not a written one.

THE PUBLISHERS

THE THIRD YEAR

BY November, 1941, the United States was all but at war. The Lend-lease act, which permitted the shipment of arms and materials to England, had been signed in March. After she entered the war against the Axis, Russia was made a beneficiary and was now receiving useful contributions at Murmansk in the far north and through Iran in the south. The U. S. Navy was patrolling the Atlantic in an effort to insure the delivery of this material. Several American merchantmen had been sunk by German U-boats, and two U. S. destroyers had been torpedoed.

Tension between the United States and Japan, ascendant since 1940, had now reached the critical stage. The U. S. State Department was demanding two explanations from Japan. Specifically, why she was massing troops in French Indo-China and, generally, what was her future policy regarding China. Special Japanese envoy, Saburo Kurusu came to the United States in mid-November with a portfolio full of replies.

But the real answer came on Dec. 7, the "day of infamy", when 200 aircraft carrier-borne planes attacked the American fleet and installations at Pearl Harbor. Simultaneously, Japan struck at the Philippines, Hong-Kong, Thailand, and the Malay States. Japan's entire campaign in the Pacific was based on crippling the U. S. fleet at Pearl Harbor. Judged strictly on its military merits, the "sneak attack" was entirely successful. One battleship was lost and seven others so severely damaged that they were out of service for months to come.

Japan's early progress was rapid. On Jan. 2, 1942, Manila fell, and General Douglas MacArthur's forces retired to the Bataan Peninsula to begin their historic delaying tactics. The battle for Malaya was won on Feb. 15 when Singapore surrendered. By March 1, the Netherlands Indies, with Sumatra, Borneo, and Celebes gone, were still carrying on with Java as the last stronghold. Japan had already invaded Burma, capturing Moulmein, Feb. 1, and then Rangoon, the entry port of the Burma Road, March 9.

Against the dark picture of Japanese victories in the Pacific was silhouetted the brighter situation on the Russian front. Starting in late November, 1941, and aided by the Russian winter, Soviet troops had staged a great recovery. In the south, Rostov had been retaken, and, in the north, the sieges of Leningrad and Moscow relieved. On March 1, 1942, the Russians were driving the Germans before them towards White Russia and exacting a heavy toll in manpower and equipment as they advanced.

FALL OF THE NETHERLANDS INDIES

IN late February, the Japanese launched an all out attack against Java. The fate of the island was sealed in a naval battle in the Java Sea, Feb. 27 to March 1. In this engagement the combined U. S. and Dutch fleets lost 13 cruisers and destroyers, practically their full complement, and were no longer able to prevent Japanese landings on Java. Batavia fell on March 5 and by March 10 all resistance had ended.

With the Netherlands Indies conquered, the Japanese high command directed its efforts in three spearheads. One pushed on through Burma, another attacked New Guinea in a preliminary drive on Australia, and the third was catapulted at the Philippines in an effort to crack the Bataan defenses. The Burma drive was still progressing in late April with the Japanese approaching India's border. Great Britain, concerned with the threat to India, had offered this nation dominion status in exchange for military cooperation. The proposal was rejected by India's leaders.

In New Guinea, the Japanese established a beachhead at Salamaua, March 8, from which they began an advance on Port Moresby. Reinforced Allied air strength, based on Australia, pounded the Japanese base at Salamaua and Rabaul on Britain—which had been previously captured. The menace to Australia seemed at least temporarily checked in late April.

After holding off a sustained three week attack by picked Japanese troops, the defenders on Bataan were compelled to capitulate on April 9. Several thousand American and Filipino troops escaped to Corregidor Island where they surrendered on May 6, after ammunition and food supplies became exhausted.

On Jan. 2, twenty-six nations had signed the United Nations Pact at Washington. This agreement called for a unanimity of purpose and action against the Axis Powers. Each signer pledged his country's full resources in the pursuit of the war and agreed no separate peace was to be made.

By May there were definite signs that the United Nations were gaining in strength. To block Japanese control of the Indian Ocean, British forces landed on the French island colony of Madagascar. After a short campaign the Vichy-French forces were subdued and the danger averted that Madagascar might go the way of French Indo-China.

On the night of May 30-31, Great Britain launched the first great air attack on Germany. Over 1000 bombers blasted Cologne in a raid that razed much of the city and destroyed many of its vital war industries. The raid on Cologne was the first of the prodigious air assaults on German soil that were to continue for the next two years and which were expected to provide a minor second front action.

CORAL SEA AND MIDWAY

THE advance of the Japanese in the South Pacific was finally halted by two great and critical naval battles. On May 4 a strong American fleet composed of aircraft carriers and escorting ships contacted a large Japanese fleet cruising in the Coral Sea towards Australia. In an engagement that lasted until May 7, and one that was unique in that the opposing fleets never were within gun range of one another, American carrier-borne planes sunk fifteen Japanese warships including one large carrier. The American losses were one carrier (Lexington), one destroyer and one tanker.

On June 4, a large flotilla of Japanese warships and transports arrived off Midway Island and began an air attack that was obviously a preliminary move on Pearl Harbor. Midway's land based aircraft stopped the assault on the island and forced the Japanese fleet to withdraw. An American fleet, stationed in the vicinity in anticipation of such an enemy thrust, pursued the Japanese and administered a crushing naval defeat that altered the whole course of war in the Pacific. When the battle ended on June 7, American bombers had sunk four carriers, two cruisers and three destroyers, and had

damaged three battleships and four cruisers, as well as a number of lighter ships. The American fleet suffered the loss of the carrier "Yorktown" and a destroyer. Midway was similar to the Coral Sea engagement in that distances prohibited surface vessel fire and the damages sustained on both sides resulted from air action.

LIBYAN ACTION

IN LIBYA the picture for the United Nations was not so bright. After the British had pushed the Italians out of Egypt in the Spring of 1941, the German Afrika Korps was formed and sent to fight beside their allies. Another British offensive in November (1941) again won Bengasi by Dec. 25. At this point German General Irwin Rommel took charge of Axis fortunes in Libya and succeeded in retaking Bengasi, Jan. 29, 1942. A new phase of the see-saw battle of Cyrenaica began in May when the British started another westward thrust which showed much promise in the early weeks. But Rommel soon outmaneuvered the British, took Tobruk, which they had held through all their adversities, and slashed his way into Egypt. He took Matruh, the Egyptian fortress, July 1, and advanced until he reached El Alamein, only 70 miles from Alexandria, the British naval base. At El Alamein the British braced and the battleweary Afrika Korps were unable to get to Alexandria and the Suez Canal.

The long awaited second German offensive into Russia started in early June. Nazi forces took Sevastopol, July 2, and Rostov, July 28, and then drove two spearheads, one at Stalingrad, which came under siege in mid-August, and the second at the oil-laden Caucasus region.

THE SOLOMONS

AMERICAN marines opened their campaign to take the Japanese occupied Solomon Islands on August 7. The first assaults were at Florida, Tulagi, and then Guadalcanal. The landing operations were supported by fleet action during which the Americans lost four cruisers in the naval battle of Savo Island on the night of August 9. Within a few days, the Marines captured the Japanese built airfield on Guadalcanal (Henderson Field) and the long struggle for the Solomons and the protection of the Allied supply lines was under way.

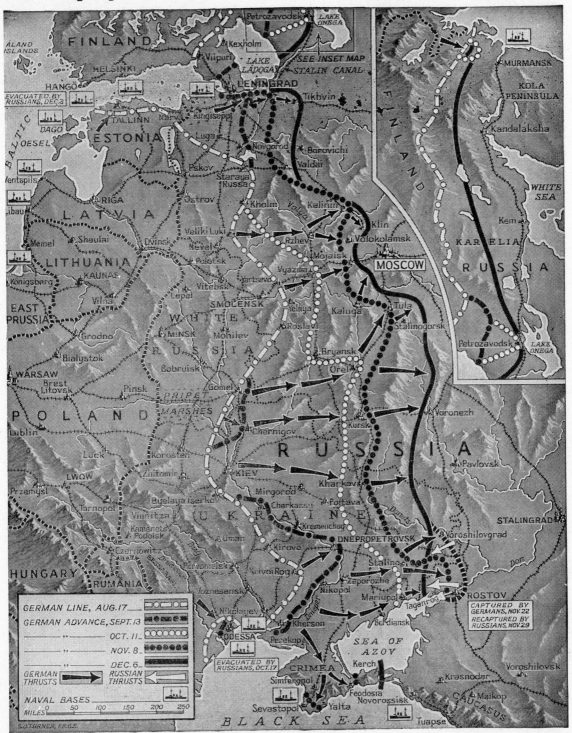

THE EASTERN FRONT AS THE THIRD YEAR OPENED. Map showing stages of the German advances in Russia from August 17 to December 6, when the offensive was brought to a standstill. During this period the most serious threats to Leningrad, Moscow and the Caucasus developed and the Russians were forced to evacuate some of their most valuable industrial towns. Losses on both sides, both in men and material, were tremendous, but the Russians held on and forced a dreaded winter campaign.

The Nazis smash along the road to Leningrad

LENINGRAD IN DANGER. After capturing Novgorod on August 27 and the Estonian town of Tallinn on September 2, the German forces attacking Leningrad pressed on to Luga, which they reached on the 3d. Here violent Russian counter-attacks momentarily stayed their advance. In accordance with an order from Hitler to take the city at all costs, however, General von Leeb threw masses of fresh men and material into the battle, regardless of huge losses, and on September 7 the German High Command announced that mobile divisions with strong air support had reached the River Neva on a broad front and had captured Schusselburg, twenty-five miles east of the city. This, together with the Finnish thrusts on the

Karelian Isthmus and between Lakes Ladoga and Onega completely cut off Leningrad from outside communication. Meanwhile, in the city itself the whole population was mobilized ready if necesssary to defend their homes to the last. The photographs show: left, a Russian armored train, its A.A. guns ready for instant action, on its way to the front line; top right, German infantry entering a blazing village, set on fire by the Russians before withdrawing; bottom, right, Russian peasants who have been forced to leave their homes in a town that has just been occupied by the Germans take their children and a few personal belongings with them as they try to find sanctuary from the Nazi invaders.

German brutality in occupied Russia

GERMANS HANG RUSSIAN CIVILIANS. The many reports of German brutality in the occupied towns and villages in Russia are strikingly confirmed by this remarkable series of photographs found on a dead German officer. They illustrate the callous hanging of five Russian civilians near the town of Velizh, in the

Smolensk region, in September, and show: (1) The victims being paraded before an officer who is sentencing them to death; (2) Climbing on to the platform of the gibbet for a soldier to fix the nooses round their necks; (3) Nazi soldiers about to remove the platform; (4) Bodies of the five victims after the hanging.

Britain's biggest bombers raid Berlin in Force

BRITAIN'S GROWING AIR OFFENSIVE. On September 7, the first anniversary of the first German mass attack on London, a strong bomber force, which included Britain's latest four-engined Stirlings and Halifaxes, gave Berlin its heaviest bombing of the war so far. The raid, which was carried out in bright moonlight, lasted for two hours and extensive damage was caused to buildings, factories, warehouses and railway

yards. The weight of the attack was shown by the German Press, which called the raid "one of the most rotten and disgusting ever made on Berlin." The Berlin raid, together with raids on Kiel and Boulogne cost the R.A.F. twenty bombers. The pictures show: left, a Stirling crew watching their aircraft being bombed up ready for the night's operations; top, right, a Halifax heavy bomber in flight; below, a formation of Stirlings.

The Commandos pay a visit to Spitzbergen

ALLIED LANDING IN THE ARCTIC CIRCLE. On September 8 a landing on Spitzbergen was made by a mixed force of British, Canadian and Norwegian troops under Canadian command. The object of the landing was to prevent the Nazis from using the island's coal supplies, since it had become known that they had planned to seize all the coal. The operation was carried out unopposed; all the mines were completely destroyed, and all the inhabitants—some 700 miners and their families—were brought back to Britain where men of military age enlisted with the Royal Norwegian forces. Spitzbergen, which lies 240

miles north of Norway within the Arctic circle, had been completely cut off from ts parent state ever since the German occupation of Norway in April, 1940, and although not actually occupied by the enemy, German mining experts were known to have paid several visits to the island in order to examine its potentialities. The pictures show: top, left, plant and machinery at a mining power station put out of action by British sappers; bottom, left, miners and their families, with their luggage and personal belongings, about to embark in the landing barges; right, fuel dumps blazing as the Allied force prepared to re-embark.

SUBMARINE SURRENDERS TO A BOMBER. On September 8, The British Admiralty announced that a German U-Boat had been attacked in the Atlantic by a Hudson reconnaisance bomber and forced to surrender. After radioing for naval and air relief, the Hudson guarded her prey for three and a half hours until a Catalina flying boat arrived to take over. After seven more hours, naval vessels arrived and took the submarine into port. The picture shows a British officer in a Carley float approaching the submarine.

TANK BATTLES IN THE UKRAINE. While the battle for Leningrad continued unabated, the Russian armies farther south counter-attacked fiercely in the Smolensk and Gomel areas thereby seriously threatening the German flanks. In order to relieve this pressure the enemy opened a new attack on Kiev which resulted in the fall of Chernigov, to the north of the city, on the 12th and of Kremenchug, on the Dnieper, on the 14th. The German tanks seen above are advancing through heavy Russian artillery fire towards objectives in the Ukraine.

Tank battle in progress on the Ukrainian Plains

GERMAN TANKS GO FORWARD. During the fighting in the Ukraine, where the vast plains offered ideal country for tank warfare, the Germans threw masses of armored vehicles into the battle. Against these the

Russians employed dive bombers and artillery, as well as their own armored forces. The picture of a tank battle in progress shows German tanks advancing through an artillery barrage from Russian batteries.

The Nazis drive on in Russia

SEPTEMBER, 1941. German infantry are here seen passing at the double through a blazing Russian village which has been "scorched" by its inhabitants. Scenes such as this were common on all parts of the Russian front during the German advance.

GERMANS ENTER UKRAINIAN CAPITAL. After crossing the Dnieper at Kremenchug the forces of von Runstedt switched northwards and linked up with those of von Bock advancing southwards from Chernigov. This maneuver completely encircled the capital together with large bodies of Russian troops. As a result the evacuation of Kiev was carried out on September 19, leaving the Russian armies to fight their way out of the German ring. Above, two German soldiers are seen looking out across the captured city from the citadel.

GERMANS ENTER BURNING KIEV. Before the Russians evacuated the Ukrainian capital they carried out a systematic and thorough demolition of all plants and buildings likely to be of use to the enemy. A picture of the city as the Russians left it is shown above.

The flames of war scorch the Ukrainian capital

THE GERMANS FIND A BLAZING KIEV. These dramatic pictures of the Ukrainian capital as the Russians left it, show: top, a party of German troops assaulting a Russian position on the outskirts of the city prior to their entry into the town; below, buildings in the center of Kiev left blazing by the retreating Russians; right, German soldiers in one of the city's main thoroughfares watching a burning building.

BRITISH DEPORT NAZIS IN IRAN. After the Anglo-Russian occupation of Iran in August, the Iranian Government agreed to close all enemy legations and to hand over enemy nationals for internment. There was considerable delay, however, in carrying out these demands, and, as a result of strong protests by Britain and Russia, the Shah abdicated on September 16 and was succeeded by his son. As many enemy nationals were still hiding in the country, British and Russian troops advanced to the outskirts of Teheran on the 17th, and on the 18th Soviet parachute troops occupied the airfields and barracks in the vicinity. The next day all the remaining Germans who had been sheltering in the legation were deported. The pictures show: above, British armored cars en route to the capital; luggage of the Germans being removed.

BRITISH SUCCESS IN ABYSSINIA. After the fall of Amba Alagi, in May, the only remaining Italian resistance in the country was centered around Gondar. On September 28, however, British and native forces attacked and captured the Italian garrison of Wolshefit, an important position guarding Gondar from the north. The Italian commander, Colonial Gonella, his staff, and 3,000 troops were taken prisoner, and the way was paved for an assault upon Gondar itself. The pictures show: above, Colonel Gonella with his men receiving full military honors; below, some of the Italian colonial troops who took part in the battle.

AIR ATTACK ON BRITISH BATTLESHIP. On September 30, the British Admiralty announced that an important convoy had been attacked by Italian aircraft in the Mediterranean. Escorting naval forces accounted for thirteen enemy planes by putting up a terrific barrage from which only one attacker escaped. During a second attack the battleship Nelson was hit by a torpedo, but only slightly damaged. The attacker was shot down. The photograph shows the enemy plane actually attacking; the splash on the right is the torpedo hitting the water. The burst of shells from the Nelson's A.A. guns are clearly visible.

A BAD BREAK FOR THE WOUNDED. On October 6, negotiations for the exchange of seriously wounded prisoners of war broke down after a first batch of Germans had been embarked. The ships should have left on October 4 for Dieppe, where they would have taken on British prisoners for the return journey. Negotiations which were conducted by radio failed because Germany, at the last moment, insisted on the exchange being made on a purely numerical basis. Above, the hospital ships, brilliantly illuminated, are at their dock waiting to depart, while below, Medical Corps men carry out a disembarkation rehearsal.

543

Russians bomb the Finns on the Karelian front

THE BATTLE FOR LENINGRAD. Throughout September the battle for Leningrad continued with undiminished violence, but despite the fact that the Germans, in accordance with Hitler's orders to take the city at all costs, threw masses of men into the line regardless of loss, they were unable to break through the

strong Russian defenses. Early in October, Russian counter-attacks, south, east and west of the city forced the Nazis on the defensive, while in the Karelian Isthmus, where the Finns were threatening the city, severe casualties were inflicted. Above, a town on the Karelian Isthmus after an attack by Russian bombers.

The German steam roller advances on the Caucasus

RUSSIANS LOSE MARIUPOL AND BERDIANSK. The German crossing of the Dnieper at Kremenchug was a serious threat to the Russian armies in the Ukraine. Not only did it help to bring about the fall of Kiev, but it threatened the whole of the Russian defenses on the east bank of the Dnieper and made it imperative that they should straighten, and consequently shorten, their line. In addition, the enemy succeeded in ferrying troops across the wide lower reaches of the river under strong aerial protection, and in pushing on towards the Crimea. On September 25 fierce fighting was reported at Kherson, and a few days later the enemy had

reached the Perekop Isthmus and was endeavoring to force his way into the Crimea. Meanwhile another thrust along the shores of the Sea of Azov pushed the Russians back to Berdiansk and Mariupol, which fell on October 6 and 14 respectively. Farther north, where the great industrial city of Kharkov was threatened, the Russians launched counter-attacks, particularly in the Kursk area, with the object of relieving the enemy pressure. The pictures show: left, German infantry, supported by tanks, in action in the streets of Mariupol; right, the destruction of the railway station which was dynamited by Russians just before the evacuation.

Moscow begins to feel the grip of the Nazi pincers

RUSSIAN CAPITAL HOLDS OUT. The third German drive towards Moscow began on October 1 with pincer thrusts in the Roslavl and Kholm areas. By the 7th the enemy were in Orel and were exerting heavy pressure near Bryansk and Vyazma which resulted in the fall of these towns on the 12th and 13th respectively. Two days later a German column penetrated as far as Mojaisk, but was driven back by well-timed counter-attacks. The seriousness of the situation was admitted by the Russians who announced that the Germans

were using about 18,000 tanks on this front alone. On the 19th, after the fall of Kalinin and Kaluga, Stalin issued an Order of the Day declaring that Moscow would be defended to the last man, and at the same time a state of siege was proclaimed in the capital. The pictures show: top, left, Russian prisoners captured during the fighting at Bryansk; bottom, left, men of the Hitler Corps passing through a burnt-out village; top, right, women and children sheltering from artillery fire; bottom, right, a German tank in Vyazma.

A French port gets a going over from the R.A.F.

LE HAVRE BOMBED. During October the R.A.F. carried out almost daily attacks on objectives in enemy-occupied France. Huge four-engined Stirlings, like that seen above dodging enemy flak, took part in many of these raids, as did also Hurricane fighters equipped to carry two 250-lb. bombs. The lower picture shows an attack by Blenheims on the docks at Havre on the 15th. The numbers indicate: (1) bombs bursting on a 12,000-ton tanker moored alongside the quay; (2) a direct hit with a heavy calibre bomb on a 5,000-ton ship; (3) a near miss on a 9,500-ton vessel; (4) bombs hitting the quay; (5) damage done to a warehouse.

Odessa falls—The end of an epic siege October 16, 1941

RUSSIANS EVACUATE ODESSA. The Black Sea port of Odessa was occupied by German and Rumanian forces on October 16 after a siege that had lasted since August. The evacuation, which was carried out in perfect order, was dictated by events in the Eastern Ukraine and the consequent need of more men to reinforce the Crimea where the enemy, after crossing the Dnieper, was trying to force an entry through the narrow Perekop Isthmus. Before leaving the port the Russians destroyed all important works. The pictures show: top, citizens cheering the Russian rearguard as they moved up; below, German Panzer vehicles.

Stalino and Taganrog fall to the Nazi hordes

RUSSIANS LOSE TWO MORE TOWNS. After the fall of Mariupol on October 14, the German forces in the Ukraine, assisted by Slovak and Hungarian divisions, continued their advance, and on the 20th captured the important armaments centre of Stalino. Farther south, mechanized divisions pushing along the coast of the Sea of Azov, made progress towards the important port and communications centre of Rostov-on-Don,

beyond which lay the valuable Caucasus oilfields. On the 22nd they captured Taganrog, between Mariupol and Rostov, after many days' fierce fighting which cost them 35,000 casualties, as well as large numbers of armored vehicles, stores, and military equipment. The picture shows German troops entering Stalino; the chimneys in the background are those of a steel factory rendered useless by the Russians.

553

FALL OF KHARKOV

OCTOBER 25-29, 1941

While the German armies in Southern Ukraine were hammering their way towards Rostov-on-Don, their armies farther north were exerting all their strength to reach the great industrial town of Kharkov. The defending forces, however, by repeated counter-attacks, managed to slow down enemy progress, but were unable to bring his advance to a standstill. By the 25th enemy advanced units had entered the suburbs of the city, where fierce hand-to-hand fighting took place in the streets, which were reported to be littered with German dead. On one day alone enemy casualties amounted to 3,500 dead, but in spite of these huge losses the Germans continued to throw fresh troops into the battle and on the 29th the Russians had to abandon the city. Before the evacuation, however, all the most important factories and plants, railway rolling stock and military stores were removed and other plants that could not be got away in time were blown up. The loss of this great town was a severe blow to the Russian cause for not only was it of first importance as a manufacturing center, but it was a vital railway junction and supply center for the Russian armies covering the Donets Basin. The German victory, however, was only achieved by great loss in men and material. According to Russian sources they lost nearly 120,000 men in killed and wounded as well as 450 tanks and armored cars, nearly 3,000 trucks and more than 200 guns. The picture shows German troops, with tank support, fighting in the streets just before the town was abandoned by the Russian forces.

TWO MORE TOWNS FALL. Although the German offensive against the Crimea opened on September 27, it was not until October 28 that the enemy succeeded in penetrating the Russian defenses on the Perekop Isthmus and gaining a foothold. On November 1, Simferopol, thirty miles from Sevastopol fell, and two days later Feodosia. The picture shows German infantry leaving a trench to launch an attack.

THIRTY MILES FROM SEVASTOPOL. When the Nazis succeeded in penetrating the Russian defenses on the Perekop Isthmus, they succeeded in dividing the defending armies into two groups, one of which retired towards the great naval base of Sevastopol and the other towards Kerch. On November 1, Simferopol fell, and above, German motorized units pass through the town after the surrender.

The aircraft carrier Ark Royal goes down in the Mediterranean

LAST MOMENTS OF A FAMOUS SHIP. On November 14, the British Admiralty announced that the 23,000 ton aircraft carrier H. M. S. Ark Royal had been sunk in the Mediterranean by a torpedo from a U-boat. Efforts were made to tow the ship into port, but she developed a heavy list and foundered before she reached her destination. Out of a complement of about 1,600 only one man was lost. The picture shows a British destroyer taking off the crew of the doomed ship before she foundered.

LOG OF THE ARK ROYAL. H. M. S. Ark Royal, most famous of all British aircraft carriers, was the third ship of this type to be lost since the war opened. During her career on active service she had steamed some 205,000 miles and engaged in thirty-two operations. She served in the Norwegian campaign, participated in the hunt for the Graf Spee and her aircraft torpedoed the German pocket battleship Bismarck on May 28. Both Italians and Germans claimed to have sunk her on several occasions.

The United States arms her merchant ships

NEUTRALITY ACT REVISED. In view of the frequency of Axis attacks on U.S. Ships, the Senate on November 13, recommended the amendment of Sections 2, 3, and 6 of the Neutrality Act, on the same day the House of Representatives approved. The President signed the bill on the 18th and on the same day the

Navy department announced that 300 to 400 ships would be armed immediately, first preference being given to those serving Britain and Northern Europe, and second to those operating to and from the Red Sea. Above: men are seen at work on a gun that is being fitted to a U.S. merchant ship.

Second British offensive in Libya

NOVEMBER 18, 1941

At dawn on November 18, Imperial forces under the command of Lieut.-General Sir Alan Cunningham, with strong air support, crossed the Egyptian frontier into Cyrenaica on a broad front from the coast east of Sollum to as far south as Jarabub. The object of this attack was to engage and destroy German and Italian forces who were massing on the frontier and constituting a threat to Egypt, and to regain if possible the territory which had been lost during General Rommel's advance of the previous spring. For some months before the attack was launched the British forces had been steadily reinforced with men, tanks and aircraft, many of the tanks being of American manufacture. These forces had been skilfully dispersed, and camouflage had been used to such good effect that when the advance began very little opposition was encountered either from the air or from ground forces. Pressure was rapidly exerted on Axis forces holding positions from Helafaya to Sidi Omar where British armored formations, with New Zealand, South African and Indian troops in support crossed the frontier and penetrated some fifty miles into enemy territory. The R.A.F., and the Australian and South African Air Forces, gave strong support to the troops on the ground, and during the day destroyed between them eighteen Axis aircraft besides bombing enemy transport on the Benina road, near Benghazi. The picture shows a line of British tanks moving out to attack the enemy.

Opening phases of the British advance in Libya

BRITISH CAPTURE

In the evening of November 19, British advance forces captured Sidi Rezegh, southeast of Tobruk, and on the following day battle was joined with strong German armored forces. After losing seventy tanks, thirty-three armored cars and several hundred prisoners the Germans withdrew. On the 21st a heavy tank battle began in the Sidi Rezegh-Gabr Saleh-Capuzzo triangle, but Gen. Cunningham was able to in-

SIDI REZEGH

terpose his forces between the main German tank strength to the east and a smaller force to the west. The enemy made three attempts to break through, but was driven back with heavy losses. The pictures show: top, enemy tanks ablaze; left, a knocked-out German tank, left, below a British column moving across an enemy minefield; right, captured German guns; right, below, troops negotiating barbed wire.

American-built planes see action in the desert

TOMAHAWKS TO THE RESCUE. The tank battle around Sidi Rezegh continued until November 28, when there was a pause. During this time General Rommel had been trying, without success, to break through the British ring and effect a junction with his troops to the west. Sidi Rezegh itself changed hands several times. Meanwhile New Zealand infantry pushing westwards along the coast occupied Bardia on the 22nd and Gambut on the 23rd, and on the 27th succeeded in linking up at El Duda with a force that had sallied out from Tobruk. During the next few days these troops gradually widened their corridor of contact, but

on the 29th the Sidi Rezegh battle flared up once more. After several unsuccessful attempts to break through to the west, Rommel concentrated all his available tanks on a narrow front and on December 1 succeeded in hammering his way through the Tobruk corridor by sheer weight of armor. The R.A.F. and R.A.A.F. played a prominent part in these operations, bombing enemy communications and harassing his ground forces with machine gun and cannon fire. The fighter pilots in the above picture are members of an Australian Squadron using American-built planes. They are on their way to take the air.

Conquest of Abyssinia complete

NOVEMBER 27, 1941

Just before dawn on November 27 an intense artillery bombardment was opened up on Gondar, last remaining centre of Italian resistance in Abyssinia, and the town was heavily bombed from the air. This was followed soon after daybreak by a general assault from several directions by British, Empire and Allied Forces under the command of Major General C. C. Fowkes. After capturing the advanced enemy positions at Deffeccia and Maldiba, Gondar itself was stormed by East African troops who, by the evening, had gained complete control of the town. At 6 p. m. the Italian commander, General Nasi, surrendered with all his forces, amounting to about 10,000 men, half of whom were Italians. This victory brought the campaign in East Africa to a successful conclusion. The pictures show: top, Italian prisoners marching through Gondar under escort; left, men of the King's African Rifles marching past the saluting point during a ceremonial parade held to celebrate the victory in Abyssinia.

Germans driven back in South Russia

ROSTOV LOST

After the fall of Taganrog on October 22 the Russian forces on the southern front retreated slowly towards Rostov-on-Don, about forty miles farther east. This town owes its importance to its navigational facilities and its position on three key railways. The Russians employed skilful delaying tactics and blew up the Don dykes thereby inundating large tracts of country between the town and the Sea of Azov. In addition Soviet guerrillas were especially active behind the enemy lines. Nevertheless, on November 22, just a month after the fall of Taganrog, the Germans entered the town. Their victory, however, was short lived. On

...AND REGAINED

the 28th, the Soviet 57th Army, commanded by General Remizov, re-entered Rostov from the south-west and on the following day the 9th Army fought its way into the town from the north-west, thereby practically encircling the Germans who, after two days of fierce street fighting in which they lost more than 5,000 men killed, beat a disorganized retreat. The pictures show: top, German troops passing through Taganrog, where factories and other buildings are blazing furiously; left, Russian soldiers hunting down German stragglers in Rostov; right, citizens welcoming Russian troops when they re-entered the town.

German drive towards Moscow halted at the gates

GERMANS AT THE GATES OF MOSCOW. The great German bid to take Moscow continued unabated throughout October and November, but the enemy made slow progress. Klin and Volokolamsk fell on November 26 and 28 respectively, but strong counter-attacks near Tula and Klin upset the German plans to encircle the capital. Early in December the enemy threw every available man and tank into a gigantic frontal attack; Mojaisk fell on the 6th and advance units actually penetrated to within about thirty miles of the capital after some of the bloodiest fighting of the campaign. But they got no farther. Thereafter the initiative passed steadily into Russian hands as winter's icy grip descended upon the scene of battle. The pictures show: top, left, Moscow citizens digging anti-tank ditches at the approaches to the city; below, left, Cossack cavalry attacking an enemy position near the city on foot; above, ill-clad German soldiers, only one of whom is wearing an overcoat, with horse transport, retreating north of Moscow; below, a big Russian tank passing through the capital on its way to the front line only a few miles away.

Pearl Harbor: Japan declares war on the United States

JAPAN ENTERS THE WAR IN TRUE AXIS FASHION. At dawn on the morning of Sunday, December 7, 1941, a force of about 150 Japanese bombers and torpedo-carrying planes launched a surprise attack on Pearl Harbor, the chief U.S. Naval base in the Pacific. Hits were scored on several naval craft lying at anchor in the harbor and two battleships, the Oklahoma and the Arizona were sunk. Other military objec-

tives on the island, including Hickam Field, U.S. Army air base, were attacked and considerable damage was done. The casualties amounted to 4,500, 2,300 of which were fatal. It was not until later in the day that the formal declaration of war against America and Great Britain was made. The above picture, **one of the best combat photographs of all time**, shows the magazine of the U.S.S. Shaw exploding.

Pearl Harbor: Five U.S. battleships stricken from the air

DESTRUCTION ON A SUNDAY MORNING. Japan's entry into the war, although sudden, was not unexpected. Ever since the previous October when the direction of Japan's foreign policy had fallen into the hands of the military clique under the leadership of General Tojo, that country's relations with the United States and Britain had steadily grown worse. The new premier had demanded a free hand to liquidate the "China Incident" once and for all, and had declared that until America and Britain refrained from supplying arms to China and recognized Japan's leadership in the Western Pacific no peaceful settlement was likely to be reached. On November 14, however, a special envoy, Saburo Kurusu, arrived in Washington to aid Admiral Nomura, Japanese Ambassador, in the latter's talks with the United States government. Three days later General Tojo announced a three-point program upon which, he said, the success of these negotiations depended. The points were: (1) Third powers must re-

frain from obstructing the successful conclusion of the China affair; (2) countries surrounding Japan must refrain from presenting a military menace to the empire and must end all economic blockades and (3) must exert their utmost efforts to prevent an extension of the European war to East Asia. On December 6 President Roosevelt sent a personal note to the Emperor of Japan, but before any reply was received, and while the Washington talks were still proceeding the attack on Pearl Harbor announced that Japan had entered the war in true Axis fashion by striking first and declaring war afterwards. Testifying to the extent of the Japanese attack on December 7, as shown in picture at left, left to right, the U.S.S. West Virginia, severely damaged, U.S.S. Tennessee damaged and the U.S.S. Arizona sunk. In the picture at right, alongside of the U.S.S. Oklahoma (far right) which capsized, the 31,500-ton U.S.S. Maryland was damaged slightly and was one of the first ships to rejoin the fleet after the Japanese attack. In addition to the damage to warships, Hickam Field, the Army Air Field outside of Honolulu, and a large floating drydock were blasted to wreckage. On the same day the Japanese occupied the International Settlement at Shanghai.

PEARL HARBOR. The U.S.S. California settles into the mud of Pearl Harbor. Clouds of smoke conceal all but the hull of the capsized U.S.S. Oklahoma, far right. The next day, Monday, December 8, the United States and Great Britain formally declared war on Japan. In the United States President Roosevelt addressed a joint session of Congress after which a resolution was introduced in both houses and adopted with one dissenting vote. Three days later Germany and Italy declared war on the United States and on the same day the challenge was accepted by the American people.

DRYDOCK AT PEARL HARBOR. The jumbled mass of wreckage in the foreground of the drydock are the U.S. destroyers Downes (left) and Cassin (right). The battleship in the rear is the U.S.S. Pennsylvania, flagship of the Pacific fleet, which suffered relatively light damage from the Japanese attack. Main and auxiliary fittings of the Downes and Cassin are being transferred to new hulls.

SIEGE OF SEVASTOPOL. After capturing Feodosia, the German forces in the Crimea drove eastwards and on November 16 captured the town of Kerch thereby compelling the Russian forces to carry out a hazardous withdrawal across the Kerch straits. Meanwhile, on the west of the Crimea, the enemy had thrown three armored and nine infantry divisions against the defenses of the great Russan naval base of Sevastopol, but the Russian line held firm and tremendous losses were inflicted upon the attackers.

The picture shows parents who have just found the body of their son who was killed in the Crimea.

RECAPTURE OF TIKHVIN. Although the Germans succeeded in encircling Leningrad, their efforts to take it by storm failed. Nevertheless, during October and November, they pushed slowly eastwards and on November 29 captured Tikhvin, 100 miles south-east of the city. On December 8, however, Russian forces under General Merezhkov re-entered the town after a battle in which more than 7,000 Germans were killed and much valuable war material was captured intact. The pictures show: above, German horse and mechanized units in retreat; below, Russian infantry following up a tank attack.

Sinking of the British battleships Prince of Wales and Repulse

JAPANESE LAUNCH ATTACK ON MALAYA. On December 8 a fleet of Japanese transports, with strong naval support, approached the mouth of the Kelantan River, North-East Malaya, and landings were carried out north of Kota Bahru. On the same day a British Naval force which was steaming to intercept the enemy convoy was heavily attacked with bombs and torpedoes by a strong force of Japanese bombers.

The Prince of Wales and the Repulse were hit several times and sunk. At the time of the attack the ships were without aerial protection owing to enemy attacks on the airfields from which their land-based air-craft operated. Casualties amounted to 595 officers and men, among whom was Admiral Sir Thomas (Tom Thumb) Phillips. The picture by the British artist, Frank Mason, shows the height of the attack.

Japanese effect a landing in the Philippines

CAVITE IN FLAMES. At daybreak on December 10 strong Japanese forces, with heavy naval and aerial protection, attempted landings on the west coast of Luzon, in the Philippines, between Vigan and San Fernando, but were repulsed by American and Filipino troops, and three enemy transports were destroyed by U.S. Aircraft. Some parachutists who had been dropped near Vigan were rounded up. Later in the day, however, fresh Japanese troops, in considerable force, established themselves at Aparri, on the northern

tip of the island, and attempted to push southwards, heavily engaged by the defenders. During the day Manila, the chief town of Luzon and capital of the Philippine Islands, was twice raided by waves of Japanese bombers; attacks were made on the Nichols airfield and Fort William McKinley, and considerable damage was done at the naval base of Cavite, on Manilla Bay, eight miles south-west of the capital; where 200 bombs were dropped, killing thirty and injuring 300 persons. Above: the water front ablaze after a raid.

Another "Napoleon" retreats before Moscow

GERMANS RETREAT BEFORE MOSCOW. After bringing the German offensive to a standstill on December 6, the Russian armies defending Moscow launched strong counter-attacks all along the line. On the 15th, after a week's fierce fighting, they recaptured Klin, and on the same day Kalinin itself was in their hands. In the center of the line heavy pressure was exerted near Mojaisk, while to the south of

the capital, strong thrusts forced the enemy back to Kaluga, which fell on the 30th after changing hands several times. The pictures show: top, abandoned German guns and vehicles left behind by the enemy during their retreat from Klin; left, well-clad Russian soldiers advancing through a village on the Moscow front which has recently been cleared of the enemy; right, buildings in Kalinin set on fire by the Nazis.

German battleships at Brest feel the fury of the R.A.F.

HALIFAX AIRCRAFT OVER TARGET

GNEISENAU

SCHARNHORST

DAYLIGHT RAID ON BREST. Ever since March, when the German battle cruisers Scharnhorst and Gneisenau entered the harbor at Brest to refuel after a raiding expedition in the Atlantic, these ships had been repeatedly attacked by the R.A.F., and several direct hits scored. In May they were rejoined by the heavy cruiser Prinz Eugen which had managed to reach port after the action in which the Bismarck was sunk. Attacks on these three valuable ships continued throughout the year, and the fact that they

PRINZ EUGEN

were unable to put to sea showed that they had suffered considerable damage. On December 18 a particularly heavy daylight attack was made on these ships by Sterling, Halifax and Manchester bombers, strongly escorted by Spitfire and Hurricane squadrons. A great weight of bombs was dropped and direct hits were scored on the dry docks in which the ships were berthed. Five British bombers and one fighter were lost against an enemy loss of eight fighters Above, bombers are seen over the target during the raid.

GERMAN RETREAT IN LIBYA. After breaking out of the ring which British forces had thrown around them, the Germans in Libya retreated rapidly, pursued by mobile columns and harassed by bombers and low-flying fighters which inflicted severe damage to their closely-packed formations. On December 19 Derna and Mekili were entered without opposition, and by the following day advance British troops were within eighty miles of Benghazi and still advancing. Above, a heavily loaded Indian transport column is seen passing through Derna with supplies and equipment for the troops in the forward areas.

FIGHTING IN LUZON. After the failure of their initial attempt to gain control of the Philippines, the Japanese, on December 22, landed a force of about 100,000 men, together with tanks, in the Lingayen Gulf area of Luzon. Landings were also made on Mindanao, the second largest island of the group, where fighting took place in the Davao area. On this day, too, the small garrison of 400 Marines at Wake Island, the U.S. naval base, 3,000 miles to the north-east, surrendered after an heroic defense lasting fourteen days. The pictures above show ruins of San Pablo, near Manila, after a severe raid on Christmas Day.

The capital of Cyrenaica falls to the British

BOMB BURSTS

SHELL BURSTS FROM GUNS OF ATTACKING FIGHTERS

FALL OF BENGHAZI. After capturing Derna, the Eighth Army continued its pursuit of the retreating enemy forces. The main German Army was in the Soluk area, south-east of Benghazi, while Italians were concentrated along the coast north-east of the town. On December 21 British forces captured Cirene and Apollonia and exerted strong pressure on the Italians covering Benghazi, and on the next day mobile columns reached the coastal plain on the Gulf of Sirte. On Christmas Eve Benghazi was entered by the Royal Dragoons after it had been evacuated by the enemy, and the nearby airfield of Barce was captured by Indian troops. On the same day a mixed mobile column occupied Benina. With the fall of Benghazi the whole of Cyrenaica, except for the isolated enemy garrisons at Sollum, Helafaya and Bardia came under British control. Pictures show: top, Axis column under fire; left, bombs falling on the airfield; right, sunken Axis ships.

AXIS MOTORISED
COLUMN

DEFENSE OF THE ISLANDS. One of the big guns on Corregidor, the fortified rock in Manila Harbor, which inflicted severe damage on the Japanese before the gallant defenders succumbed to the constant pounding of the enemy. American and Filipino forces continued to resist the invader from this fortress long after Manila was evacuated but outnumbered and exhausted were forced to surrender on May 6, 1942.

NON-MILITARY OBJECTIVES. In the picture at top, a whole row of houses in the residential section of Pasay are shown leveled by Japanese bombs, while (below), residents of Cavite are evacuating the town after the raid of December 10 in which 200 bombs were dropped and thirty persons were killed.

HAVOC AND WOUNDED. The smoking ruins of the town of San Pablo, 35 miles from Manila, bear testimony to the effectiveness of Japanese bombs, while below, a group of wounded Filipinos are shown as they awaited medical attention in a dressing station speedily set up by volunteers.

THE CAPITAL IS BOMBED. In the picture (top) fires set by Japanese bombs are shown as they swept the Intramuros, Manila's famous walled city, while below, a residential section is shown after it was bombed mercilessly by the Prussians of the Orient. On the morning of December 10 the capital was twice raided by Japanese bombers and attacks were made and considerable damage done to Nichols airfield and Fort William McKinley, headquarters of the American Army on the island.

Second British offensive in Libya—Advance of Eighth Army

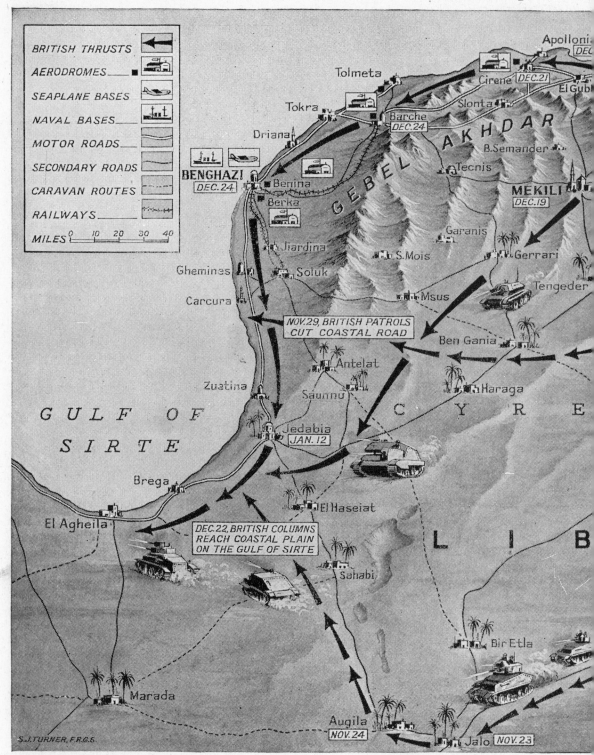

ADVANCE OF THE EIGHTH ARMY. Map showing the stages of the second British and Imperial advance in Libya from the opening of the offensive on November 18 until January 17 on which date the Axis garrison at Helafaya surrendered. By this time the whole of Libya had been cleared of enemy forces except for a

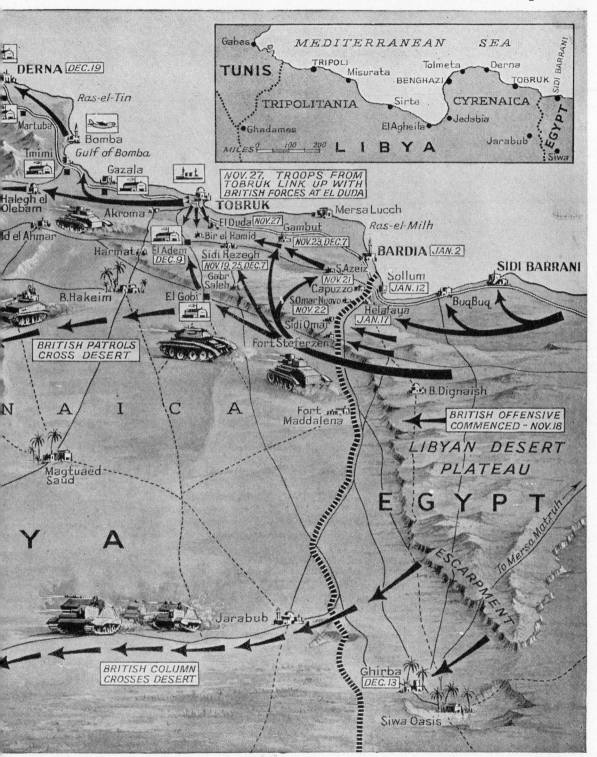

pocket of resistance in the El Agheila area which was being strenuously attacked. During these operations a German and Italian army of more than 100,000 men had been notably defeated, and much of its equipment destroyed. Axis air losses during the first six weeks amounted to 467 aircraft against a British loss of 195.

JAPANESE SUCCESS IN CHINA. On Christmas Day, after resisting Japanese attacks for seven days, and rejecting three demands to surrender, the British colony of Hong Kong capitulated. Under the leadership of Sir Mark Young, the Governor, the garrison of British, Canadian and Indian troops, had fought heroically against overwhelming odds and continual artillery and air bombardment. The decision to surrender was only taken after important reservoirs had fallen into enemy hands and there was one day's supply of water left. The picture shows Japanese artillery in action in the suburbs just before the garrison surrendered.

ATTACK ON ENEMY SHIPPING. On December 27, British forces landed on the coast of Norway at Maaloy and Vaagso Islands. Coast defenses were silenced by British warships and bombers and commandos were landed under cover of smoke screens. The operation resulted in the destruction of 15,560 tons of enemy shipping in addition to munition dumps, oil tanks and military stores. The pictures show: above, an oil factory at Vaagso ablaze after having been blown up by British sappers and below, a commando on a height overlooking Maaloy, where the garrison were killed or taken prisoner. All British ships returned safely.

Pounding away at Bardia

A BIG GUN ROARS. Bardia, a small town on the north coast of Libya, was subjected to terrific bombardments from naval, land and air forces during the campaigns of 1940, 1941. Captured by the British on January 5, 1941, it was retaken by Axis forces on April 13, 1942. After the British launched their successful offensive in November, 1941, Axis troops in Bardia held out long after the main British assault had passed westward, but fell on January 2, 1942. In the picture at right, a heavy field gun is shown pounding away at the Axis-held town, just before the desert stronghold fell to the British.

RUSSIANS RETAKE TWO TOWNS. On December 30 Russian forces of the Caucasus command, with strong support from the Black Sea Fleet and the Red Air Force, crossed the Kerch Straights into the Crimea and after fierce fighting captured the towns of Kerch and Feodosia which had been occupied by the Germans in November. Cossack troops who played a prominent part in these operations are seen (above) bringing up machine guns in face of heavy enemy artillery fire; and, below, waiting to attack en enemy blockhouse.

JAPANESE ADVANCE IN LUZON. On December 31 American and Filipino forces faced with overwhelmingly superior numbers of enemy troops, backed by tanks and dive bombers, were forced to evacuate Manila and Cavite and fall back to shorter lines. The island fortress of Corregidor, at the entrance to Manila Bay, continued to hold out. Japanese forces entered the capital (above) at 3 p.m., where they found all military stores destroyed. Below the city of Intramuros, the old section of Manila, ablaze after an air attack.

Charging across the hot sands of the desert

ADVANCE. In this unusual picture, British infantrymen are shown advancing at the double across the open desert outside the seaport of Tobruk, during one of the phases of the battle of Libya during Great Britain's

second offensive. Imperial troops had been steadily reinformed with men from the dominions and American tanks and aircraft. Pressure was rapidly exerted on the Axis forces holding positions in the desert.

Ready to repulse air attack in the western desert

ON THE ALERT. Anti-Aircraft gunners rush to their posts as word is received of approaching Nazi planes from one of the Axis controlled air bases during the height of the battle for Libya. While the axis forces had

control of the air during this phase of the engagement, British anti-aircraft gunners had very good success and were able to bring down hundreds of the enemy planes at a small loss in men and equipment.

Japanese drive for Singapore gains momentum

JUNGLE WARFARE IN MALAYA. After carrying out landings in Northern Malaya early in December, the Japanese launched strong assaults on the British positions with light tanks and armored vehicles, supported by masses of dive bombers. Further landings on the coast behind the British lines seriously threatened the defenders' flanks and forced them to carry out a series of tactical withdrawals in face of strong enemy pressure. By these tactics the Japanese gained control of the northern aerodromes and were able to concentrate overwhelming air superiority on all sectors of the front. By December 17, Penang, on the west coast, had

been evacuated, and on the 29th the mining town of Ipoh was in Japanese hands. On January 7 the enemy launched a strong offensive in Lower Perak in which he used 12-ton tanks to crash his way through the British lines. As a result Kuala Lampur, capital of the Federated Malay States, was evacuated on the 11th. The pictures show: left, enemy tanks and motor vehicles on a jungle road on fire after being engaged by anti-tank guns; in the lower picture one of the crew lies dead beside his tank; right, above, British anti-tank gunners firing at enemy tanks, and, (below), a close-up of a knocked-out tank with its dead crew by its side.

Bardia, Sollum and Helafaya surrender to the Allies

AXIS GARRISONS SURRENDER. The town of Bardia, which had been occupied by the New Zealanders on November 22 and reoccupied by the enemy on December 1, surrendered unconditionally to British and Imperial forces on January 2 after a brilliant attack in which Polish and Free French forces took part. More than 7,000 Axis prisoners were taken, including Major-General Schmidt, administrative head of the Afrika Korps. British casualties were only sixty killed and 300 wounded. Having reduced Bardia, the British forces turned

their attention to the strong enemy positions covering Helafaya, last remaining pocket of enemy resistance in E. Cyrenaica. On the 12th they captured Sollum and five days later Helafaya itself surrendered after putting up a stiff resistance. Here a further 5,500 prisoners were taken, together with large quantities of guns and material. The pictures show: above, Axis prisoners outside Bardia waiting to be taken to prison camps; top, left, some of the 300 prisoners captured at Sollum; below, left, Axis surrender at Helafaya

ASSAULT ON MOJAISK. Hooded Russian infantry, clad from head to foot in white to make them invisible against the snow, are here seen approaching Mojaisk during the final stages of the Russian assault on the town.

RUSSIANS RECAPTURE MOJAISK. Although the Russians had succeeded in driving the Germans out of Klin, Kalinin and Kaluga, thereby removing the pincer threat to Moscow from the north and south, the enemy forces in Mojaisk, in the centre, fought desperately to retain this important position which they had won at great cost on December 6. On January 15, the Russians launched their assault on the town and after bitter street fighting in which the Germans defended themselves house by house, the Nazis were forced to retreat and the town which Hitler had ordered his troops to hold at all costs was recaptured.

Japanese advance into Burma gets under way

FIGHTING BEGINS IN BURMA. On January 20, Japanese and Thai forces crossed the frontier into Burma, and fighting occurred north of Myawaddi, sixty miles east of Moulmein. In face of a numerically superior enemy the British forces were obliged to fall slowly back towards Moulmein. The enemy used strong air

forces to support his offensive, but fighters of the R.A.F. and the American Volunteer Group inflicted heavy losses on the raiders. Above, Japanese infantry, some of whom are equipped with cycles, are seen crossing a river by a temporary bridge, the main structure having been destroyed by the British before they retired.

AUSTRALIA THREATENED. After a Japanese landing on Sarawak on December 16, the British forces withdrew, on January 1, to Dutch Borneo, where they joined up with Netherlands troops. On the 10th, however, the enemy landed at Tarakan, Dutch Borneo, and also on North Celebes. The oil installations at Tarakan were destroyed by the Dutch before they were forced to surrender on the 13th. On January 22, after fresh enemy landings, the oil wells at Balikpapan, on the east coast, were destroyed to prevent them falling into enemy hands. On the same day landings were carried out on New Ireland and at Rabaul, capital of New

Britain, in the Bismarck Archipelago, thereby threatening New Guinea and bringing the war dangerously close to Australia. On the 23rd, heavy Japanese air raids were made on Lae, New Guinea, which was evacuated after the attack. The pictures on the left show: above, blazing hangars at the airfield at Salamaua, not far from Lae, after a heavy Japanese raid; and below, the Balikpapan oil wells blazing furiously after their voluntary destruction by the Dutch forces. The radioed pictures above, show: top, a Japanese landing party somewhere in the Pacific; and below, warships putting up a smoke screen to cover a landing by Japanese.

A NEW A.E.F. PREPARES FOR ACTION. On January 26 the first U.S. troops to land in Britain since 1918 disembarked at a Northern Ireland port. They formed the vanguard of the American Expeditionary Forces to Europe, and they had been convoyed safely across the Atlantic by British and American warships. After disembarking, the troops marched to camps that had been prepared for their arrival and soon they were getting into battle trim by strenuous maneuvers over rough country. The pictures show: above, U.S. gun teams practicing with British artillery and below, infantry following heavy tanks during a mock attack.

The retreat to Singapore—Malaya evacuated January 30-31, 1942

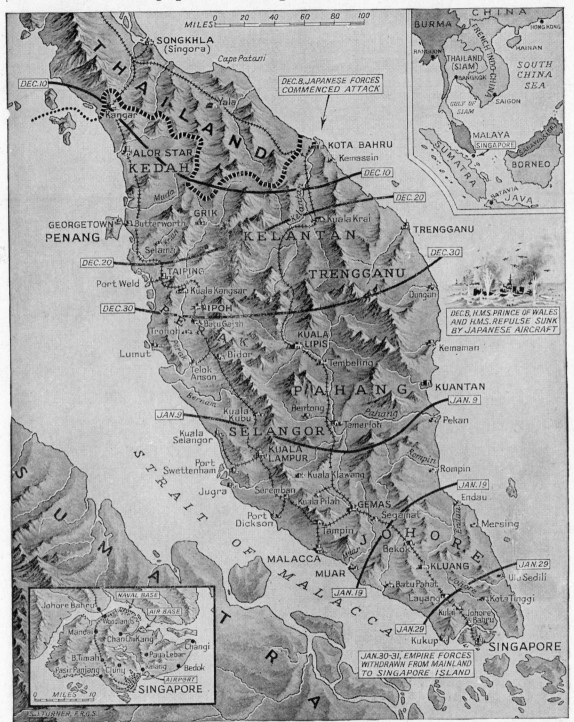

BRITISH SET-BACK. After a fighting retreat in the face of a numerically superior enemy who had almost undisputed control of the air, all the British forces on the Malayan mainland were withdrawn to Singapore Island on the night of January 30-31. The operation was covered by a stand south of Kulai by three Highland regiments who inflicted heavy casualties on the enemy. After the withdrawal the Causeway linking the island with the mainland was blown up. The map shows the stages of the Japanese advance, with inset of Malaya in relation to surrounding territory, and Singapore Island.

The U.S. Navy raids the Marshall and Gilbert Islands

U.S. NAVY HITS BACK. On February 1, a brilliant surprise attack was carried out on Japanese naval and air bases in the Marshall and Gilbert Islands by a U.S. force of aircraft carriers supported by cruisers and destroyers. Heavy damage was caused to enemy ships and harbor installations and many planes were destroyed on the ground. The Japanese losses amounted to one light cruiser, a destroyer, two submarines, a 17,000 ton liner, three 10,000 ton tankers, five 5,000 ton cargo ships, two fleet auxiliaries and two minesweepers, amounting in all to some 100,000 tons. In addition at least eight more ships, amounting to about 50,000

tons, were severely damaged. Thirty-eight enemy aircraft were destroyed in combat for a loss of eleven U.S. planes. The air bases at Taroa, Wotje, Roy and Enybor were wiped out. No U.S. vessel was lost. The pictures, taken during these operations, show: top, a U.S. naval plane over Wotje Atoll, the columns of smoke come from ammunition and fuel dumps that have been set on fire. Left, an American cruiser and aircraft carrier during the action; the latter has just been narrowly missed by a Japanese bomb. Right, the flight deck to one of the aircraft carriers with its aircraft lined up on the deck ready to take off.

LANDINGS ON SINGAPORE ISLAND. After the British retired across the Causeway from Johore Bahru to Singapore Island on January 31, there was a brief lull in the siege during which time the Japanese forces on the mainland reorganized for the final assault on the island fortress, which opened on the night of February 8 and by the 12th the invaders were near the racetrack, two miles north-west of the city, and the reservoir, only source of Singapore's water supply was seriously threatened. The pictures show: top, Japanese light tanks at the Johore end of the Causeway and below, Japanese trucks crossing an improvised bridge to Singapore Island, built to replace the damaged Causeway.

The "key to the Pacific" falls to the Japanese February 15, 1942

SINGAPORE SURRENDERS. The capital of the Straits Settlements fell to the invaders on February 15, after a siege of fifteen days. Thus ended the campaign in Malaya which had lasted for seventy days and had been fought against a numerically superior enemy, who from the outset, had almost undisputed control of the air. The pictures show, top, a damaged British ship in the docks at Singapore during a bombing attack, and bottom, burning buildings and warehouses on the waterfront. In the center picture Japanese infantry and tanks in action on the outskirts of the city.

Japanese continue their advance in Burma

FALL OF PEGU. On January 30 the Japanese forces in Burma occupied Moulmein and the British retired to the west bank of the Salween river. On February 10, however, the enemy crossed the river north-west of Martaban and after fierce fighting occupied the town. Farther north other attempts to cross the river in the Paan area were repulsed, but on the 15th, the British were withdrawn to the line of the Bilin river after evacuating Thaton. Here strong counter-attacks, in which the R.A.F., the Indian Air Force and the American Volunteer Group gave valuable support, slowed down the Japanese advance, but on the 22nd a fresh attack

was mounted by the enemy who forced a crossing of the Bilin and made heavy assaults on a bridgehead on the east bank of the Sittang river, the next obstacle in their way. The town of Pegu, forty miles north of Rangoon, fell, and the railway from Rangoon to Mandalay and the road to China were thereby cut. The pictures show: above, left, General Yamashita, Japanese commander in Malaya and Burma, on a tour of occupied territory; and right, Japanese troops passing through a Burmese village; below, left, a Japanese tank column crossing a river over an emergency bridge; and right, the R.A.F. taking off from a Burmese airfield.

Russians encircle German 16th army at Staraya Russia

RUSSIAN ATTEMPT TO RELIEVE LENINGRAD. On February 23, the twenty-fourth anniversary of the creation of the Red Army, Russian forces launched an offensive on the Central Front and on the same day the High Command announced the capture of Dorogobuzh, fifty miles east of Smolensk. Farther north, where the Russians were striving desperately to break the German ring around Leningrad, Soviet troops, on the 24th, successfully accomplished the encirclement of the German 16th Army at Staraya Russa, ten miles south of

Lake Ilmen. After the refusal of the German commander to surrender, the Russians began an attack in which two German infantry divisions and the crack S.S. "Death's Head" Division were smashed and 12,000 Germans were killed. Nevertheless, the enemy, heartened by promises of airborne reinforcemnts, clung desperately to their positions. The pictures show: left, German infantry waiting in the snow beside their guns in readiness for an attack; and right, Russian sappers clearing a passage through enemy wire.

BURMESE CAPITAL THREAT-ENED. In view of the proximity of Japanese forces to Rangoon, a curfew was imposed and a military governor appointed, on February 25 in order to prevent looting. On the same day the R.A.F. and the American Volunteer Group scored a notable success by shooting down thirty Japanese bombers attempting to raid the capital. Meanwhile, in India, the evacuation of part of the Chittagong district, on the shores of the Bay of Bengal, was carried out as a precautionary measure. The pictures show: above, natives examining bomb damage in a main Rangoon street following a heavy Japanese air raid; and left, a grief-stricken Burman, whose wife has just been killed by a fragment from a Japanese bomb, clutching his little child closely to his side.

Combined attack on the coast of France February 27-28, 1942

RADIOLOCATION STATION WRECKED. On the night of February 27-28, the British Army, Navy and R.A.F. carried out a combined attack on an important German radiolocation station at Bruneval, on the French coast twelve miles north of Le Havre. Parachute troops dropped by R.A.F. bombers carried out the demolition, despite heavy enemy resistance, and the station was entirely wrecked. Infantry units landed from the sea by light naval forces covered the embarkation of the airborne forces. Heavy casualties were inflicted on the Germans and a number of prisoners were taken. No British ships or aircraft were lost. The pictures show: above, British parachute troops about to enter their aircraft, and below, landing barges returning to their bases after the raid.

DEADLY ACCURACY OF THE R.A.F. BOMBING. After the R.A.F. attack on the Renault factory at Billancourt on the night of March 3, the Germans claimed that most of the damage had been done to residences. This was disproved shortly after the raid by a remarkable series of photographs, one of which is

reproduced above, that was smuggled out of France. This shows a tangled mass of girders and machinery, all that was left of one of the factory's main workshops. In this building crankshafts, valves and motors were made. The loss of this factory was a serious blow to German war production.

GERMAN SUPPLY BASE CAPTURED. On March 5 Soviet forces under General Golubov recaptured Yukhnov, 125 miles east of Smolensk, an important rail center and supply base for the German armies on the Central Front. The town, which was protected by a formidable double row of fortifications, fell after a fierce struggle lasting several days, during which Soviet troops fought their way through the battered streets and engaged in house-to-house fighting. The pictures show: above, a Soviet Scouts Company, the first to enter the town, advancing cautiously through the ruined streets; and below, camouflaged infantry mopping-up.

DAYLIGHT ATTACK ON MATFORD WORKS. Five days after the heavy night attack on the Renault factory, a small formation of American-built Boston light bombers carried out a daring low-level daylight attack on the Matford works at Poissy, ten miles north-west of Paris, which was producing twenty trucks a day for the German Army. The picture taken from one of the attacking bombers during the height of the raid, shows bombs bursting in the center of the factory. Hits were also scored on the rows of parked trucks which can be seen in rear. Never before had British bombers penetrated so far into occupied France in daylight.

Japanese enter a scorched capital of Burma

FALL OF RANGOON. As a result of the isolation of part of the British forces at Pegu, and Japanese landings on the Irrawaddy Delta, the city of Rangoon, capital of Burma, was evacuated on March 7, and on the following day the Japanese entered the town. The British forces, despite heavy casualties, remained intact after the Pegu fighting and withdrew into Central Burma with the object of linking up with the Chinese armies farther north. Before the evacuation of Rangoon the "scorched earth" policy was thoroughly carried out; all dock installations, oil refineries and machinery that could not be removed were systematically destroyed. The photograph, taken from one of the last ships to leave the port, shows the dense clouds of oil

smoke rising from the Burma Oil Company's warehouses that have been set on fire to prevent them falling into enemy hands. On the same day as the evacuation of Rangoon, Japanese forces who had landed in Java on March 1 occupied Batavia, the capital, and three days later Surabaya, the Dutch naval base, and the city of Bandoeng, were in enemy hands, the latter having surrendered to prevent an aerial massacre of the civilian population. With the fall of these towns the fighting in Java came to an end. The gallant Dutch had lost most of their navy in trying to prevent the enemy landings, and their air force was no match for the masses of aircraft the enemy were able to use. The Japanese used at least ten divisions in the fighting.

British and Chinese armies try to turn the tide of battle

BRITISH AND CHINESE CONTACT IN BURMA After the fall of Rangoon Lieutenant-General Sir Harold Alexander took over command in Burma from General Hutton. Under his leadership the British forces withdrew northwards and on March 12 linked up with a powerful Chinese force that had marched 800 miles from Yunnan. On the 19th the enemy began to push northwards towards Toungoo, on the Sittang, and towards Prome, on the Irrawaddy, with the result that the British were obliged to evacuate Tharawaddy, on the Rangoon-Prone railway, on the 20th. At Pyu, thirty-five miles south of Toungoo, the Japanese came up against strong Chi-

nese resistance, but by an outflanking movement they managed to capture the airfield north of Toungoo and cut the Toungoo-Mandalay road, and on the 25th they occupied Kyungon, north-west of the town, thereby almost encircling the Chinese. The Chinese held Toungoo until the 31st, when they fought their way out of the trap and rejoined their main forces to the north-west. The pictures above show: left, Chinese forces passing through a Burmese village on their way to the battlefront; and right, digging anti-tank ditches in the jungle. Below, left, a camouflaged Chinese sniper in action; and right, a lightly-clad infantryman is on the double in the jungle.

Australian and American flyers attack Japanese shipping

PORT ENGINE
FALLING INTO
SEA

ALLIED AIR SUCCESSES IN THE PACIFIC. On March 18 the U.S. Navy Department gave details of successes obtained by American and Australian airmen in operations against the Japanese forces invading New Guinea. These included the sinking of two heavy cruisers, damage to three light cruisers, five transports gutted by fire and beached as well as damage to other miscellaneous craft. In all twenty-three enemy ships were sunk or damaged for the loss of one Allied aircraft. On the 19th considerable Japanese forces in New Guinea were seen advancing across the island in a south-westerly direction, but attacks by U.S. bombers on Lae and on Rabaul, where a heavy cruiser was sunk, so interfered with the enemy's plans that he was obliged, at least temporarily, to call a halt. Tokio admitted that at Rabaul alone they had sustained 7,000 casualties. The pictures show the end of a Japanese twin-engined bomber that attempted to attack a U.S. naval force in the Pacific. It is seen over a U.S. destroyer (1) shortly before it received a direct hit on its port engine, which broke off and fell into the sea (2). The aircraft immediately went into a steep dive (3) and crashed into the sea in flames (4). The crew of three perished.

Progress of the war in the Pacific after three months

PACIFIC THEATRE OF WAR. This map shows the progress of the war in the Pacific from the outbreak of hostilities to the Japanese occupation of the Andaman Islands on March 23, 1942. During that time the whole of Malaya had been overrun, Borneo, Java, Sumatra and Celebes had been occupied, and fighting was in progress in New Guinea where Japanese landings had taken place after the enemy occupation of the ad-

PRINCIPAL NAVAL BASES

BRITISH | AMERICAN | RUSSIAN | DUTCH | JAPANESE

MAIN OILFIELDS | TERRITORY OCCUPIED BY JAPANESE

joining islands of New Britain and New Ireland. American and Filipino forces in the Philippines were still resisting the enemy who had gained control of the greater part of the islands. The U.S. naval bases of Guam and Wake had fallen early in the campaign. On the Burmese front British forces were retreating before a numerically superior enemy in the direction of Mandalay. Japan's entry cut the supply route to Russia.

LUEBECK BOMBED
MARCH 28, 29, 1942

On the night of March 28, a strong force of heavy bombers gave the Baltic port of Luebeck, thirty-five miles north of Hamburg, one of the heaviest bombings experienced by any German city so far. The port handles nearly all the traffic between Germany and Sweden, and large imports of iron ore and other raw materials pass through it on their way to feed Germany's war industries. In addition it was being used for the dispatch of military stores to Finland and to the German armies on the northern front, as well as to the army of occupation in Norway. The fact that it was also an important centre of U-boat construction and a training depot for submarine crews made it an extremely desirable target for the R.A.F.'s attention.

The attack was pressed home with great determination, and soon after it began, fires could be seen dotted all over the city. These rapidly spread until it looked as if there was only one huge fire. Very heavy damage was done, and it was estimated that about 1,500 houses were destroyed, mostly by fire. The photograph below shows a section of the centre of the city stretching over 1,500 yards. In this area the Central Electric Station, the Market Hall and the Reich Bank were all completely gutted, and a close inspection of the picture shows that there is scarcely a building in the whole area retaining its roof. The picture on the left shows chaos caused by bombs in Breitstrasse.

Russians smash German attack on the Kalinin front

GERMAN ATTACK FAILS. On March 24, the Germans launched the biggest attack on the Kalinin front since the Battle of Moscow. Its object was to relieve a deep salient in their lines near Rzhev, where two large bodies of their troops had been isolated. For this purpose they employed three divisions and large numbers of tanks and aircraft, but after five days' fighting they were obliged to call the attack off, having lost 2,500 men in killed alone. Meanwhile, near Staraya Russa, the Germans were still trying desperately

to relieve their Sixteenth Army which had now been reduced by almost half. On the Leningrad front the Red Army was trying hard to free the encircled city before the thaw cut the supply line across the ice on Lake Ladoga, while in the Ukraine they had reached the suburbs of Stalino, which they had lost on October 20, and were fighting desperately to regain possession of the town. The picture shows a Russian battlefield after the tide of war has passed over it; dead bodies and burnt-out tanks litter the ground.

British destroyer rams dock gates at St. Nazaire

RAID ON ENEMY INSTALLATIONS. In the early hours of March 28, a combined raid was carried out by British naval forces and commandos against the large dry dock and harbor installations at St. Nazaire. H.M.S. Campbeltown, carrying five tons of high explosives in her specially stiffened bows, crashed through the harbor boom defenses and charged the dock entrance at full speed. Such was the impact that she forced herself into the lock entrance as far as her bridge, where, after most of her crew had

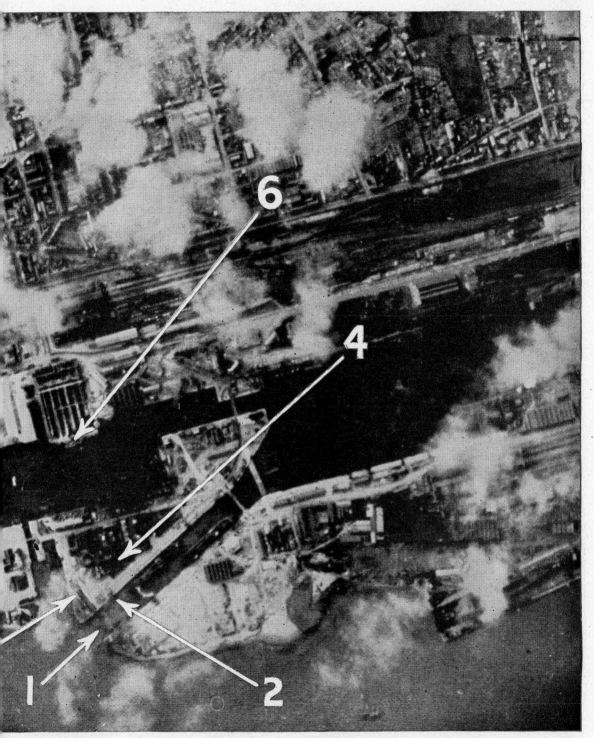

been taken off she blew up. Meanwhile commandos set about demolishing works, as shown above: (1) The dry dock, outer gate of which is missing. It was here that the Campbeltown blew up; (2) Severe damage to the dock pump house; (3) Damage to the machine house for operating dock gate; (4) Two sheds of the pump house completely demolished; (5) A five-bay building almost destroyed; (6) Damage to submarine pens under construction; (7) One end of a multi-bay building badly damaged.

FROM BATAAN TO AUSTRALIA. In the latter part of March, 1942, it was announced that General Douglas MacArthur, hero of the Philippine campaign, had arrived in Australia by air to assume command of all land, naval and air forces in the south-west Pacific. At the same time it was revealed that for two months a steady stream of U.S. soldiers and flyers had been pouring into Australia and that U.S. troops were stationed at Darwin. In the picture above, General MacArthur, right, is shown with Lieut. General Jonathan Wainwright, then a Major General, who succeeded him as Philippine commander.

MacARTHUR'S SON AT CORREGIDOR. The first picture to come out of the Philippines of Arthur Mac-Arthur, son of the General, in his soldier's uniform, in the tunnel entrance on Corregidor, with his Filipino attendant, a few days before he flew to Australia with his mother to join his father. For the MacArthurs the Philippines were more than a battle assignment. The Philippines are in their blood. The General's father, young hero of the Civil War, was military governor of the islands 45 years ago. His mother died there and under Manila's tropic palms he courted his second wife and fathered his sturdy young son.

HANDLING DYNAMITE. The Filipino soldier in center foreground is distributing sticks of dynamite to some fellow defenders of the island. The bridge was destroyed to slow the Japanese advance and was one of the many efforts made by the natives to check the foe during the months of horror brought on by the invaders. These Filipino soldiers had been schooled in the American way of armed combat by General Douglas MacArthur, who had served for years as Marshal of the Philippine Army. How well these soldiers fought against the Nipponese was revealed by all American officers on the island and their work was of the greatest value to the Americans during the dark days of the invasion and retreat to Corregidor. Like their American comrades, practically all of the Filipinos that survived the campaign were taken prisoner after the fall of Corregidor, and subjected to horrible torture.

The Japanese bomb Kipling's Mandalay March 31-April 3, 1942

FIGHTING RETREAT IN BURMA. After evacuating Toungoo the Chinese forces, now reorganized north of the town, launched a determined counter-attack, and on April 2, succeeded in recapturing Kyungon, which the enemy had occupied on March 25. Meanwhile, on the Irrawaddy front, Japanese forces in considerable strength penetrated the British positions south of Prome and on April 2, after an all-night battle, occupied the town. This brought them to within 120 miles of the important oilfields at Yenang Yaung, which was one of their main objectives. On April 3 Japanese aircraft bombed Mandalay in the heaviest raid of the Far East war to date. It was estimated that about two-thirds of the business area was destroyed and that more than 2,000 persons were killed. The picture shows damage in a Moslem quarter.

Allied air attack on Japanese-held capital of New Guinea

AIRFIELD AT RABAUL BOMBED. Smoke rolling from burning Japanese planes on Vunakanau airfield at Rabaul, New Britain, as allied bombers made the heaviest attack of the Pacific war up to that time on the Japanese-held base. One hundred and seventy-seven planes were destroyed or damaged in the raid. Note the explosion near Japanese plane in the revetment in the foreground. This operation was one of many intended to end the threat of Japanese domination of allied lines of communication in the Pacific and the north coast of Australia, the enemy having exploited his successes on the Malayan Peninsula to bring the entire Netherlands East Indies under his domination. The effects of the desperate resistance offered by the Philippine Army and United States forces on Bataan, holding as they did a sizeable portion of Japanese strength, were now being felt. During the delay thus gained men and materials were dispatched to Australia, New Caledonia and other Pacific islands. The growth of power of the United Nations in the southwest Pacific was presaged by our air forces which were now performing long-range bombing missions against Japan's newly acquired bases in the Bismarcks and New Guinea.

Heroic Malta has its 2,000th air raid alert

MALTA DEFIES THE LUFTWAFFE. The island of Malta, which stands on the direct sea route from Italy to North Africa and from which attacks were carried out by British aircraft on Axis convoys carrying reinforcements to General Rommel in Libya, was the subject of almost non-stop attacks by German and Italian bombers. During April the enemy launched a particularly heavy offensive in order to ground British aircraft while his convoys made the dangerous crossing to North Africa, and on the 7th, Malta had

its two thousandth alert since war began. On this day alone the enemy employed about 500 aircraft on attacks on the island. According to reports from Valletta about 4,200 houses had been destroyed in the raids to date, as well as the island's Opera House, the Church and Monastery of the Sacred Heart, the Capuchin Convent Church, and the Chapel of our Lady of Lourdes. The pictures show: left, bomb damage in the center of Valetta; right, above, bombs bursting on the harbor; below, bomb bursts on the island.

End of U.S. resistance on the Bataan peninsula

END OF AN

On April 9 the U. S. and Filipino defenses on the Bataan Peninsula of Luzon were smashed by Japanese forces and an epic resistance which had lasted for four months was brought to an end. General Wainright's forces on the island amounted to 36,800 men, nearly all of whom were killed or captured, but some of them, including 3,500 U.S. Marines succeeded in escaping to the island of Corregidor, which continued to hold out. Although outnumbered six to one, the defending forces put up a magnificent resistance and succeeded in inflicting

HEROIC DEFENSE. 60,000 casualties on the enemy. It was only after they were physically exhausted by days and nights of fighting that they were finally compelled to give up. The pictures show: above, left, Japanese forces on the Peninsula passing blazing oil dumps that had been set on fire by the defenders before they surrendered, and right, some of the Japanese prisoners captured during the fighting. On the left two Japanese soldiers, killed in the fighting, are seen lying where they fell, and right, a Bataan village after it had been blasted by enemy artillery.

Marching into hell

Their tragic ordeal of privation and humiliation at the hands of the brutal Japanese began for these gaunt weary defenders of Corregidor as they surrendered to the smirking enemy. Disclosures in January, 1944, revealed that these men, part of the 12,000 captured at the rock fortress of Manila Bay, were herded together like cattle and kept without food for seven days. Then they were marched in humiliation through Manila on a long weary trek to a Japanese prison camp the weak and stumbling knocked right back into line. Those falling by the wayside being bayoneted to death by their inhuman foes, in direct violation of the Geneva Convention.

INDIAN NEGOTIATIONS FAIL.

Charged with a special mission to present the British Government's plan to solve Indian constitutional problems, Sir Stafford Cripps had arrived in New Delhi on March 23. In the Prime Minister's words, Sir Stafford "did everything in human power" to insure a successful conclusion to the negotiations, but the Congress of India rejected Great Britain's proposals for a settlement. England's firm promise of Indian independence included a self-elected government for India after the War, but Congress made an uncompromising last-minute demand for the setting up of a National Government at once. Sir Stafford Cripps pointed out to Dr. Azad, the Congress President, that this demand implied absolute dictatorship of the majority, and would break all the pledges Britain had given to the great minorities of India. Above, Sir Stafford Cripps talks to some of the Sikh leaders during his visit. Below, Gandhi (in foreground), and Pandit Nehru (between the pillars) at a meeting.

LAVAL COMES BACK TO POWER. On April 14 Berlin and Vichy announced that Pierre Laval would return to office and that Marshal Petain had decided to reconstitute the Vichy cabinet on a new basis. This reorganization was forced upon Petain by Hitler who, it was said, used the French prisoners of war in Germany and threats to starve the French people as bargaining weapons. With a pro-German head in Vichy, Hitler doubtless hoped to obtain the services of French workers for essential war work in German factories, and even to obtain the use of the French fleet, which had been disarmed under the armistice terms. The new cabinet, in which Laval held the post of Chief of Government, and the Ministries of Foreign Affairs, the Interior, and Information, was formed on the 17th. Petain retained the nominal title of Chief of State Laval's appointment led to dsiturbances in Paris and Northern France, and on the 16th, thirty-five German soldiers were killed in a troop train that was derailed near Caen. The picture above, doubtless a piece of German propaganda to prove the success of the new arrangement, shows French "volunteers" in German uniforms leaving Versailles for service on the Russian front. On the left, Marshal Petain and Laval are seen together shortly after the **new government was formed.**

SHANGRI-LA IS BORN. In April, 1942, the United States and the world at large was electrified by an announcement by President Roosevelt that American flyers had carried the Battle of the Pacific to the heart of the Japanese empire with a surprising and daring raid on miliary targets at Tokio, Yokohama, Osake, Kobe and other Rising Sun industrial centers. The dangerous mission was headed by Lieut. General James H. Doolittle, and in the picture above, one of the planes is seen soaring off the flight deck of the USS Hornet enroute to Japanese territory. Taking off in the middle of the day, flying at low altitude, the squadron of American planes led by General Doolittle, and accompanied by 79 other aviators raided the mainland. In the navy yard south of Tokio a new cruiser or battleship under construction was bombed and left in flames. "Along the coast line," said Gen. Doolittle on May 19, at Washington, when he was decorated by the President and the story of the raid was revealed, "we observed several squadrons of destroyers and some cruisers and battleships. About 25 miles to sea the rear gunners reported seeing columns of smoke rising thousands of feet in the air. One of our bombardiers strewed incendiary bombs along a quarter of a mile of aircraft factory near Nagoya. Another illuminated a tank farm. However, flying at such low altitudes made it very difficult to observe the result following the impact of the bombs. We could see the strike, but our field of vision was greatly restricted by the speed of the

To Tojo from a former friend

April 18, 1942

plane and the low altitude at which we were flying. Even so, one of our party observed a ball game in progress. The players and spectators did not start their run for cover until just as the field passed out of sight. Pilots, bombardiers and all members of the crew performed their duties with great calmness and remarkable precision. It appeared to us that practically every bomb reached the target for which it was intended. We would like to have tarried and watched the later developments of fire and explosion, but, even so, we were fortunate to receive a fairly detailed report from the excited Japanese radio broadcasts. It took them several hours to calm down to deception and accusation." He added that he had issued instructions that the Imperial Palace in Tokio was not to be bombed. In the picture above General Doolittle is shown wiring a Japanese medal to the fin of a 500-pound bomb which shortly thereafter was returned to its Nipponese makers in a blast of destruction. The ceremony took place on the deck of the carrier Hornet from which the raiders took off.

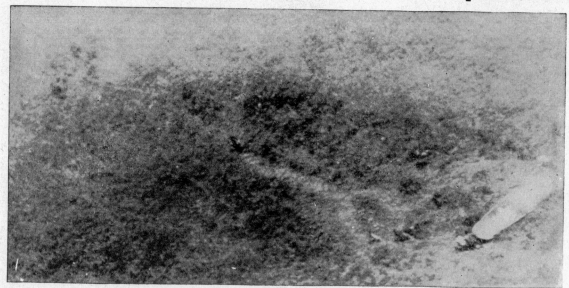

AFTER THE RAID ON TOKIO. Several planes in the squadron that took off for Tokio from the airplane carrier Hornet failed to return to the mother ship. In the picture (at top) is the wing of one of the bombers after it crashed on top of a Chinese mountain, while at bottom is another view of the wreckage. At the time of the raid there was no mention of any American losses or that any of the squadron had fallen into the hands of the Japanese, but six months later a Tokio broadcast named four of the men they were holding. It was then that the U.S. disclosed that several of the Doolittle squadron never returned.

HELP FROM AN ALLY. Chinese carry some of the Tokio raiders from the summit of the Chinese mountain where their bomber was forced down after raiding the Japanese capital. Other flyers who were shot or forced down over Japan were not so fortunate and were forced to suffer horrible forms of torture, it was revealed several months later. One of the planes landed on Russian territory and the crew was interned by Soviet authorities, the Soviet not being at war with Japan. Several of the enemy's interceptor planes were shot down by the American flyers.

GERMAN ARMY AVOIDS ANNIHILATION. On April 24, the Germans succeeded in relieving their Sixteenth Army which had been encircled near Staraya Russa in February. During the two months it had been cut off, it had been kept supplied by air, and although its numbers had been seriously depleted, it had nevertheless remained intact as a fighting unit. The picture shows German soldiers surrendering. Dead bodies of their comrades in the foreground bear witness to the doggedness of their resistance, and to their confidence in the promise, made by the German High Command, that they would be relieved.

A famous cathedral city gets a dose of bombs   April 24, 1942

FIRST OF THE BAEDEKER RAIDS. On April 24, the Luftwaffe raided the historic city of Exeter where considerable damage was inflicted on many ancient buildings and churches, including the famous cathedral, dating from 1107. This raid was followed by raids on Norwich, Bath and York, and an official spokesman in Berlin described them as reprisals for the damage done by the Royal Air Force to buildings in Luebeck and Rostock and added that the Luftwaffe would "bomb every building in Britain marked with three stars in Baedeker." Above, the cathedral is seen standing amidst the ruins of Exeter.

Reprisal raids on Exeter, Bath, Norwich and York

(1) Firemen outside St. Martin's Church, York, which was destroyed; (2) Damage in the residential quarter of Norwich; and (3) a hospital which has received a direct hit; (4) The interior of the burnt-out Guildhall, York; (5) Dam-

THE CATHEDRAL CITIES BOMBED. The raid on Exeter on April 24, was quickly followed by attacks on Bath (25 and 26), Norwich (27 and 29), and York (28), in all of which buildings and monuments of great historic value were blasted or demolished. **By**

aged houses in the center of Bath; and (6) the remains of the Regina Hotel and the Assembly Hall; (7) Interior of Exeter Cathedral, where a bomb fell on the choir aisle and demolished St. James' Chapel and the Sacristy.

choosing these undefended cities as its targets, the Luftwaffe as good as admitted that it was unable to reply on anything like the same scale to the R.A.F.'s raids on military objectives in Germany, and was forced to seek targets in lightly protected areas.

BURMA ROAD CUT. On April 19, a Japanese force estimated at five divisions (about 100,000 men), with strong tank and aerial support, began a new thrust northwards through the Shan states towards Lashio, the western terminus of the vital Burma Roard along which China was supplied with munitions of war by the Allies. In spite of desperate Chinese resistance the enemy reached Kehsi Mansam, only seventy miles south of Lashio, on the 28th, and on the following day, after a lightning advance of seventy miles, they captured Lashio itself after a mass attack which was covered by a violent artillery and aerial bar-

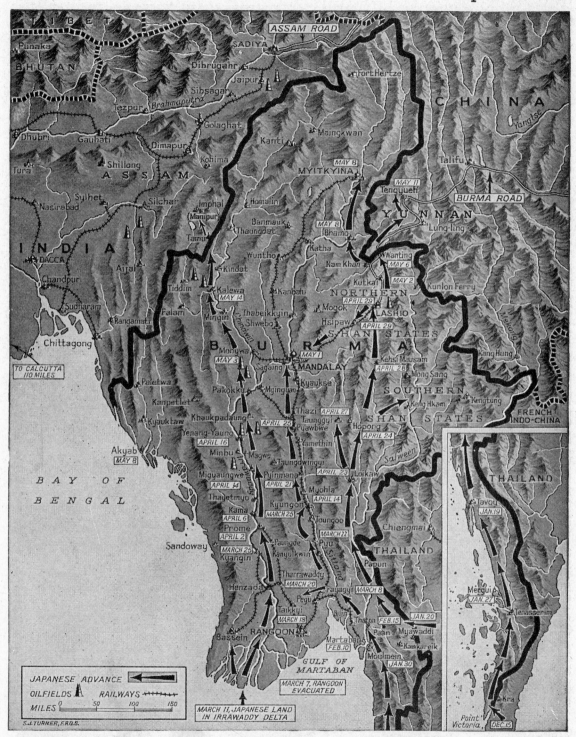

rage. On the same day the enemy captured Hsipaw, forty miles south-west of Lashio, thereby seriously threatening the rear of the Anglo-Chinese forces and, at the same time, cutting the railway to Mandalay. The pictures show: above, left, trucks, carrying gasoline and oil for the Chinese air force during a halt on the Burma Road; below, left, supply vehicles negotiating some of the hairpin bends for which the road is famous. The map shows the course of the campaign in Burma.

MANDALAY IN RUINS. After cutting the Lashio-Mandalay railway, the Japanese pressed rapidly on to Mandalay, which they occupied on May 1. The beautiful city, with its many temples and pagodas, had been almost completely destroyed by enemy bombs, and the victorious army found only a shattered ruin with all roads, bridges and military installations wrecked. The British forces were withdrawn north of the Irrawaddy, and the famous Ava Bridge across the river was blown up. The pictures show: above, damage wrought in Mandalay, and below, Japanese troops marching through a captured town.

Corregidor gives up the fight

JAPANESE LAND ON CORREGIDOR. Ever since the fall of Bataan, on April 9, the island fortress of Corregidor had been subjected to intense artillery fire at point-blank range from Japanese batteries on the mainland. This, together with heavy aerial bombardment, inflicted heavy casualties on the defenders as well as serious damage to military installations. On May 5, after a particularly severe bombardment which swept away the beach defenses, Japanese troops crossed the narrow channel separating Corregidor from the mainland and landed on the island. By the 6th the battle was over, and the gallant defenders, outnumbered and exhausted by lack of sleep, were forced to surrender. Altogether 11,574 prisoners were taken. In the picture at right, an American officer is shown giving a drink of water to a dying Japanese. A general view of the island is given below.

MARCH THROUGH THE JUNGLES. The march of Lt. General Joseph W. Stilwell and his party from Burma which started on May 1, 1942 in Burma and ended May 20, in Imphal, Assam, will go down in history as one of the great feats of an American soldier. The General, wearing old style campaign hat is shown at the head of the column, followed by Lt. Col. Frank Dorn and Lieut. Richard Young, his two aides and Major General Franklin C. Sibert. Gen. Stilwell, chief of staff to Generalissimo Chiang Kai-shek, had been in command of Chinese Fifth and Sixth Armies, operating with the British in Burma..

MARCHING ALONG TOGETHER. General Stilwell's party walking across the sands approach a river in Burma. From the time that the heroic band left Wunthe until they reached the Chindwin River the group was entirely out of touch with the world. In the spring of 1942 the Allies took what the General called a "hell of a beating" in Burma, which they lost to the Japanese, but he was still full of fight after the weary march of 140 miles through the wild Burmese jungles and the dangerous rivers and declared Burma could and would be retaken from the Japanese invaders.

THF MARCH TO INDIA. This picture, one of the most unusual pictures in military history, shows Lieut. Gen. Jospeh W. Stilwell carrying a sack of bully beef from a spit across the Uyu River to his raft. An R.A.F. plane had just dropped food to the Stilwell party and the general was one of the first into the water and carried his share of the food. The story of the Burma campaign, as Gen. Stilwell put it, was one of outnumbered forces giving the best they had against a foe with more equipment and with complete air superiority. The last a bitter pill for "Uncle Joe" to swallow.

Rivers fail to halt the march to India

MARCHING THROUGH RIVERS. For the first three days of the march through the jungles after abandoning their transport the Stilwell group walked up the murky waters of the Chaunggyi River.

A FLYING TIGER. One of the strangely decorated planes used by American and Chinese airmen under General Stilwell's command in the campaign in China and Burma.

British land in Madagascar—Diego Suarez capitulates

BRITISH OVERCOME FRENCH RESISTANCE. With the object of forestalling a Japanese move against the French island of Madagascar, which would have given the enemy a valuable base for naval and air operations in the Indian Ocean, a combined naval and military force made a landing at Courier Bay, on the western side of the island on May 5, covered by naval aircraft. The main objective was the important naval base of Diego Suarez, on the northern tip of the island, which was occupied by British forces the night of the 5th. On the 6th an at-

tack on Ansirana, on the south side of the bay, was repulsed. Later in the day British troops penetrated the town and forced the defenders to surrender. The pictures show: above, left, an invasion barge ferrying a motor ambulance to the shore; right, the British Commanders, Rear-Admiral Syfret and Major-General Sturges, inspecting British troops after the surrender. A German ship which its crew had unsuccessfully tried to scuttle is seen, below, left, in Diego Suarez harbor, and on the right are French Colonials who defended the island, later joined the Allies.

Last moments of the aircraft carrier Lexington

BATTLE OF THE CORAL SEA. On May 8, while U.S. aircraft were still in action against the Japanese fleet in the Coral Sea the enemy launched a counter-attack and scored several hits with bombs and torpedoes on the 33,000-ton U.S. Aircraft Carrier Lexington. Several hours after the battle, while steaming at 20 knots, the Lexington was rocked by a terrific internal explosion, probably caused by the ignition of gasoline vapors from leaks in the gasoline lines. As the flames grew the captain ordered the crew to abandon ship. Ninety-two percent of the ship's company were rescued and reached port safely. The last man off the ship was her commanding officer, Captain Sherman, and, as he slid down a line into the water, a torpedo in the warhead

locker exploded, and the Lexington sank soon afterwards. The picture shows the crew abandoning ship shortly after the explosion. A U.S. destroyer, which had come alongside to render assistance, can be seen through the smoke which envelops the carrier's superstructure. The U.S. attacks on Salamaua and Lae, and the Battle of the Coral Sea, besides foiling the enemy's invasion plans, cost him the aircraft carrier Ryukaku, three heavy cruisers, one light cruiser, two destroyers, and several transports sunk, a cruiser and a destroyer probably sunk, and damage to a second aircraft carrier, the Syokaku, which was hit on May 8 and left ablaze. American losses were the Lexington, the destroyer Sims, and the 25,000-ton tanker Neosho.

Russian winter advance

RUSSIAN COUNTER ATTACKS. After the failure of the German attempt to capture Moscow, the Russian armies took the offensive all along the front and drove the enemy back over a large part of the ground he had overrun. The Germans, however, succeeded in holding most of the important railheads and in clinging to their positions around Leningrad, which despite furious attacks, the Russians failed to relieve. The map shows the territory (shaded dark) recaptured during the Russian offensive at enormous cost to the Nazis.

Germans launch offensive in the Crimea May 8-16, 1942

START OF GERMAN SPRING OFFENSIVE. On May 8, German and Rumanian forces, under General von Manstein, launched a limited local offensive in the Crimea with the object of clearing that area of Russian troops and safeguarding their right flank against any possible Russian attack. In face of very strong pressure, the Soviet forces slowly withdrew, inflicting heavy casualties on the enemy as they retreated. On the 15th, the enemy penetrated the suburbs of Kerch, and on the following day they claimed to have captured the town. The pictures show: above, Russian tanks, followed by infantry, advancing through enemy shell fire during a counter-attack in the Crimea; and below, Russian troops firing at the advancing Germans.

RUSSIAN ARMIES STRIKE FIRST. In order to forestall a probable German attack, Marshal Timoshenko on May 13, launched an offensive on a fifty-mile front stretching from Chuguyev to Volchansk and quickly made deep penetrations into German defensive positions covering Kharkov. By the 15th, Russian forces had crossed the Donets and had advanced ten miles west of the river. On the 17th, in an effort to envelop Kharkov from north and south, the Russians broadened their front, which now stretched for 100 miles from

Byelgorod to Smiyev, and particularly heavy tank battles raged around the latter place, where giant Russian and American tanks scored notable successes against the enemy. Between May 12 and 16, Soviet forces liberated 300 inhabited localities in advances varying from twelve to thirty-eight miles, besides killing about 12,000 enemy troops. The pictures show: left, German machine gunners in action against the Russians, and right, a German sentry outside a factory in Kharkov that has been fired by Russian artillery.

GERMAN COUNTER-OFFENSIVE. In order to hold up the Russian drive towards Kharkov, von Bock, on May 19, launched a strong counter-offensive in the Izyum-Barenkovo area where he struck hard at the Donets River crossings. As a result he succeeded in halting the Russian push farther north, and on the 29th, Berlin announced that the Kharkov battle had ended with Kharkov still in German hands. Meanwhile, on the 23rd, the Russians had been obliged to evacuate the Kerch Peninsula and the German right flank was now secure against attack from the rear. The pictures show: above, a street in a Russian village destroyed by the advancing Germans, and below, German tank and motor-cycle reinforcements rushing up to the front line to take part in their new drive.

TWO ALLIES AFFIX THEIR SIGNATURES. On May 21, V. M. Molotov arrived in London to sign a twenty-year treaty of alliance between Great Britain and the Soviet Union. The signatories undertook to give each other military and other assistance against the Axis and agreed not to conclude a separate peace with the enemy. They also agreed to collaborate with one another and with the other United Nations in the peace settlement and during the ensuing period of reconstruction on the basis of the principles set out in the Atlantic Charter. The picture above shows, Anthony Eden, watched by Prime Minister Churchill, putting his signature to the treaty, while on his right, Mr. Molotov and Ambassador Maisky sign for the Soviet. The powerful Russian bombing plane that brought Mr. Molotov to England is seen below.

GERMAN OFFENSIVE IN LIBYA

May 26, 1942

After heavy dive bombing attacks on the British positions in Libya, General Rommel, on May 26, launched a full scale offensive with the object of defeating the British armored forces and capturing Tobruk. His plan of campaign was to capture Bir Hakeim, at the southern end of the British minefield and send the Afrika Korps, supported by German and Italian mobile divisions, round the southern end of the minefields. At the same time a holding attack was to be made on the British positions running south from Gazala to the Trigh Capuzzo. On the night of May 26, 27, Rommel carried out the first part of his plan, the Afrika Korps passing round Bir Hakeim and advancing rapidly towards Acroma and towards El Duda and Sidi Rezegh, which some of his forward troops actually reached before being driven back by British armored columns. A few enemy tanks reached the escarpment overlooking the coastal road north of Acroma, but were driven back. On the same night the enemy attempted a landing from the sea at this spot with the object of joining up with the tanks, but this was frustrated by naval forces working in close co-operation with the army. Before the Axis forces reached El Adem Acroma, they were brought to action by British mechanized divisions and turned back. The attack on the British positions between Gazala and Trigh Capuzzo, made on the 27th, was repulsed with heavy casualties and an attack on Bir Hakeim by the Italian Mobile Corps was repulsed by the Free French. The pictures, taken during the opening stages of the offensive, show: above, part of a German armored division advancing through a heavy artillery barrage put up by British batteries, and below, Axis tanks being rushed up to the main battle area to reinforce their hard-pressed forces.

German tank attack repulsed in desert battle near Tobruk

ENEMY ATTACK REPULSED. After their failure to reach Tobruk, the German tank formations which had been advancing in two columns towards El Adem and Acroma, reunited in the neighborhood of Knightsbridge, twelve miles south of Acroma, where they were engaged by British armored forces and heavy fighting developed. This continued until the 30th, the battle swaying backwards and forwards over a wide area from Acroma in the north to Bir Hakeim, and from El Adem to the British minefields. By the 30th the enemy, finding himself running short of supplies and water, forced two gaps in the British minefields and attempted to pass his forces through these. By the morning of June 1 he had succeeded in withdrawing many of his

vehicles and was bringing up guns to cover their retreat. A large number of his tanks, however, and many motorized units remained to the east of the minefield, and these were ceaselessly attacked by British troops and the R.A.F., and many of them were destroyed. It was estimated that during this period at least 600 enemy vehicles were put out of action, and in Cairo it was authoritatively stated that the Afrika Korps had taken a severe loss and that the position remained "not unfavorable" to the British. The pictures show: left, above, a mobile British anti-tank gun passing a knocked-out German tank, and below, British soldiers examining a wrecked German tank. On the right, a South African patrol is seen sheltering from enemy mortar fire.

RHINE CITY RAIDED BY R.A.F. On the night of May 30, a force of more than 1,000 bombers attacked the Ruhr and Rhineland, with Cologne as the main objective. More than 2,000 tons of bombs were dropped and it was estimated that more than 250 factory buildings and industrial plants were destroyed or severely damaged. The pictures show the workshops of the Koelnischer Gummifaden Fabrik, at Deutz, a suburb of Cologne, before and after the raid. This factory was engaged in the manufacture of tires and inner tubes.

REPRISAL FOR COLOGNE RAID. On the last night of May, a small force of enemy bombers raided Canterbury, where considerable damage was caused in the business district and many people were made homeless. The German High Command described the raid as a "reprisal for the terrorist raid on Cologne," and Berlin radio said that Canterbury, "a main centre of English hypocrisy," had to pay for the attack on the old beautiful city on the Rhine. Although no bombs hit the Cathedral, several fell nearby, causing damage by blast. The picture shows Dr. Hewlett Johnson, Dean of Canterbury, inspecting the damaged library.

695

AIRCRAFT CARRIER YORKTOWN GOES DOWN. On June 3, two large Japanese fleets approached Midway Island, U.S. naval and air base in the Pacific. As soon as the enemy's presence was reported a strong force of army bombers set out to locate the Japanese fleet and in the attack that followed direct hits were scored on eight enemy ships. Meanwhile a force of about 180 Japanese carrier-borne planes raided the airfields, docks and harbor installations on the island, but succeeded in inflicting only minor damage. The strength of the U.S. attack forced the enemy to withdraw with tremendous losses, the greatest sustained by the enemy since the war began, amounting to four aircraft carriers, two battleships damaged, two heavy cruisers sunk and three damaged, one light cruiser damaged and three destroyers sunk. U.S. losses amounted to one aircraft carrier, the Yorktown (shown above) and the destroyer Hammon. Military strategists later interpreted the attack on Midway as a preliminary thrust, the ultimate objective of which was the Hawaiian islands and the complete neutralization of the base at Pearl Harbor. The complete defeat of the Japanese fleet was the stroke that equalized the strength of the American and Japanese navies and permitted the latter to drop the defensive role imposed upon it since the outbreak of hostilities. Like the battle of the Coral Sea, the engagement at Midway was unique in naval history in that there was no exchange of fire between the big guns of the opposing fleets. At all times at least 200 miles of Pacific ocean separated the opponents. All damage was scored by bomber and torpedo planes flown from carriers, with the Americans having the additional help of land-based bombers.

Enemy action and a loss in the battle of Midway   June 3-7, 1942

ATTACK FROM THE AIR. Japanese planes in the battle of Midway attempt to attack Pacific fleet forces through heavy anti-aircraft fire. Smoke on the horizon is from an enemy bomber shot down. Splashes in the foreground are caused by falling shrapnel. This battle, described by many as the greatest sea engagement since Jutland of World War 1, practically insured the safety of the American west coast.

THE ENEMY LOSES A CRUISER. A Japanese heavy cruiser of the Mogami class after she was hit by U.S. bombs and left in a sinking condition. The battle of Midway, lasting more than three days and nights, was such a complex and widespread action, that even the active participants of the United States forces were unable to sum up thoroughly all the damage inflicted on the enemy; but it is known that approximately 4,800 Japanese were killed or drowned and that the total losses to the United States forces were 92 officers and 215 enlisted men. In tonnage, the Japanese at Midway lost more than the Germans lost in the classic battle of Jutland. Almost without exception, these losses could be attributed to ship-based United States Navy aircraft. The Battle of Midway climaxed the first six months of the United States at war and marked the opening of a new phase of operations in the Pacific—the enemy offensive had been checked.

DUTCH HARBOR RAIDED. On the morning of June 3, Japanese planes raided the U.S. naval and air base at Dutch Harbor, Unalaska, in the Aleutians. High explosives and incendiary bombs were dropped, but damage was light. A few barracks and warehouse at Fort Mears and Dutch Harbor were bombed and set afire and a Navy patrol plane, which was about to take off with mail was strafed. The picture shows bombs dropping harmlessly in the bay. The ship in background staved off the enemy attack with machine gun fire. In the harbor at the time of the attack were three United States destroyers, an army transport, a mine-sweeper and a Coast Guard cutter, and also an old station ship, The Northwestern, which had been beached and was being used as barracks. This ship was destroyed in the second attack on June 4.

DAYLIGHT RAIDS ON THE ENEMY. During June daylight attacks of increasing force were made by British and American bombers on industrial targets in Germany and the occupied countries. Early in June nearly 100 bombers of the R.A.F. made a concentrated attack on the Philips radio works at Eindhoven in Holland. This factory, the largest of its kind in Europe, was entirely engaged on production for the German armed forces. Large sections of the works were destroyed by fire. Another great raid was made on the steel works at Lille by Flying Fortresses. Over 150 tons of high explosives and a great weight of incendiaries were dropped on the main buildings within a few minutes and fierce fires were seen spreading over the whole area as the attackers flew away. Above, a German "flak-train" used as an additional means of defense against the increased Allied air attacks over the Reich and enemy occupied countries.

HEADACHE FOR THE ALLIES. In February, 1941, after brilliant successes in Europe, Lieut. Gen. Erwin Rommel was sent to Africa to head the Afrika Korps, following the rout of the Italians by the British. He began a counter-attack that covered 1,125 miles in two months and drove the British back to the Egyptian border. Early in 1942 he was made a Field Marshal and after a successful campaign was finally checked by General Sir Bernard L. Montgomery at El Alamein and driven out of Africa. This photograph of the Marshal was taken from a Nazi prisoner captured by Fifth Army forces in Italy. Rommel's record on the European continent and in Africa made him one of the outstanding generals of the war. Practically obscure before the start of hostilities in 1939, his first great success was scored during the conquest of France. It was the mechanized divisions under Rommel that breached the French line in the Sedan sector and made the famous drive towards the English channel. This operation cut off the British and Belgians from the French army and made the evacuation of Dunkirk imperative. After he was sent to Africa, Rommel's reputation grew at an even greater pace. During early 1942 he was practically unbeatable. One of his quirks was a habit of entertaining captured English officers. During these seances he took considerable pleasure in lecturing them on military tactics and pointing out to them the mistakes which caused their downfall. In 1943, Rommel nearly accomplished the supreme objective of driving a wedge to the Suez Canal, a task upon which the Italians had embarked in 1940 with little success against the British.

ACTION AT LONG RANGE. In the picture at top, British artillery are shown shelling enemy positions during the push against the Axis in Libya, while, below, British soldiers, manning a six-pounder, duck for a moment in the midst of loading their gun as an enemy shell lands close by.

A GALLANT DEFENSE NEARS ITS END. Besieged for months by Axis forces, the British garrison at Tobruk not only held out comfortably, but continually strengthened its defenses. With the harbor accessible to British merchant and naval vessels the stronghold remained a deterrent and threat to Axis columns intent on driving on toward Suez. On December 10, 1941, however, Axis columns smashed through and one of the greatest sieges in the history of the world ended. The British first captured this Libyan fortress and seaport in their 1941 drive, when the Italian garrison of 25,000 surrendered on January 22. Subsequently the Axis staged a counter-offensive and from mid-April until December 10, 1941, the British Imperial garrison, made up largely of Australians, withstood a German-Italian siege. The weary defenders were relieved when the British in their second drive across North Africa, pushed the Axis forces westward across Libya. The second siege of Tobruk lasted only four days, the port and 33,000 British prisoners falling to Marshal Rommel on June 21, 1942 in one of the war's outstanding upsets. The above picture shows British soldiers at Tobruk manning an anti-aircraft post girt by Italian ammunition boxes filled with stones.

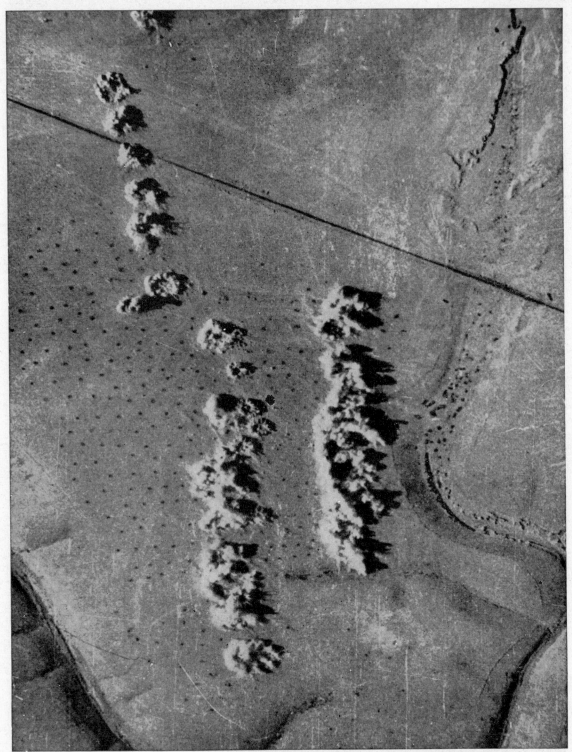

TROUBLE FOR THE AXIS. A dispersed ammunition dump in Libya is bombed by aircraft of the South African Air Force which played a conspicuous role through many campaigns during the British activity in the Western Desert. The hits can be seen clearly.

NEW GERMAN ATTACKS IN RUSSIA. The fighting in the Kharkov sector died down towards the end of May and there was a period of comparative quiet which lasted until June 10 when a fresh German attack was launched to recapture the strong points in their defenses round Kharkov taken by Marshal Timoshenko in his recent offensive. On the 25th the Russians evacuated Kupiansk, an important rail junction sixty miles southeast of Kharkov, and on the following day they had to abandon Izyum, on the Donets, the scene of the great tank battles a month earlier. The pictures show: above, Nazi tanks passing a burning church during their advance, and below, Soviet infantry riding into battle on their tanks during a counter-attack.

JAPANESE LAND AT KISKA. On June 13, the U.S. Navy Department announced that Japanese landings had taken place at Attu and Kiska, in the Aleutian Islands, 1,300 miles from the Alaskan mainland and only 600 miles from the new American naval base at Dutch Harbor. Bad weather prevented immediate action, but on the 15th, U.S. forces attacked the enemy and sank one cruiser and severely damaged three other cruisers, an aircraft carrier, a destroyer and a gunboat. A few days later a number of transports were observed at anchor in Kiska harbor and were attacked by U.S. Army bombers, which succeeded in sinking one. The picture shows the ship ablaze. Two other transports can be seen on the left and right.

GERMANS CAPTURE TOBRUK
AND MERSA MATRUH
June 18-29, 1942

After the withdrawal of the British forces to the Egyptian frontier, mobile formations harassed enemy columns pushing eastwards towards Bardia and turned them back about twenty-five miles from the town. On the 20th, however, Rommel's tank forces suddenly switched their attack towards Tobruk from the direction of El Adem and El Duda and succeeded, with the help of massed dive bomber attacks, in forcing a gap on a narrow front in the southeast perimeter defenses through which tanks and infantry passed. On the 21st, after desperate fighting, the town and port were occupied and the garrison of 25,000 was forced to surrender. On the same day the enemy occupied Bardia. By the 26th, after capturing Capuzzo, Sollum, Helafaya and Sidi Barrani, the enemy had got within fifteen miles of Mersa Matruh, and on the next day battle was joined with his main armored forces. As a result Mersa Matruh fell on the 29th and the British and Imperial forces fell back in good order. The pictures show: left, Italian infantry taking up positions prior to the Axis attack on Tobruk; left, below, some of the British troops taken prisoner in Tobruk; and right, British gunners in action before Mersa Matruh.

Black Sea naval base of Sevastopol falls to the Germans

A CITY IN RUINS. The fall of Sevastopol was a severe blow to the Russian cause. The great naval base, home of the Black Sea Fleet, was of the utmost strategic importance to the enemy, for not only did its capture remove the last remaining threat to his right flank, but it gave him a base from which he could in the future carry out landing operations south of the Caucasus Mountains. This would threaten the port of Batum and the vital oil-centre of Baku. In addition its loss would seriously restrict the free movements of the Black

Sea Fleet, which was now well within the range of enemy bombers. The defense of Sevastopol forms one of the most glorious episodes in the annals of military history, and the picture shows how the defenders heroically clung on to their positions until the whole town was reduced to a complete shambles. Those civilians who were not evacuated lived under unspeakable conditions, yet, together with the soldiers and the marines of the Black Sea Fleet, they defied the might of the invading German Army for many months.

Germans cross the Don river and open a new offensive

DEFENSE OF VORONEZH. On June 28 the Germans began a new offensive in the Kursk sector, 120 miles north of Kharkov, the object of which was to capture the important rail junction of Voronezh, on the Moscow-Rostov railway, 130 miles east of Kharkov. This would have given the Germans a strong defensive bastion on the flank of their attack farther south. By early July fighting on a tremendous scale had also developed in the Byelgorod and Volchansk areas (between Kursk and Kharkov), where thousands of tanks, closely followed by infantry and supported by masses of dive bombers, battered at the Russian positions. In face of tremendous pressure the Russian armies slowly withdrew in good order, taking terrible toll of the enemy as they retired. On July 7 the Germans succeeded in establishing bridgeheads on the east bank of the Don opposite Voronezh across which they managed to throw an infantry division and 100 tanks. The crossings,

however, were under continual fire from Russian artillery and aerial bombardment by Stormovik dive bombers, and the Russians launched repeated counter-attacks with strong forces of tanks and infantry. According to Russian reports the Don was flowing red with the blood of dead Germans. Meanwhile, farther south, the enemy was pushing eastwards in an attempt to gain control of the middle reaches of the Don. On the 8th the Russians evacuated Stary Oskol, and two days later they abandoned Rossosh after severe battles in which as many as 8,000 tanks were locked in combat on a front 110 miles long. The picture shows the ruins of a bridge across the Don blown up by the Russians in an attempt to slow up the smashing tactics of the well armed and fast-moving Nazi invaders in this new drive for territory. German troops can be seen threading their way past smashed trucks and cars, which litter the ground for miles around.

British Eighth army strikes back at El Alamein

BATTLE OF

After the fall of Mersa Matruh, Rommel continued his advance eastwards, and by July 1 he had reached El Alamein, only sixty miles from Alexandria. It was here that General Auchinleck decided to make a stand, for the country formed a narrow bottleneck, the sea guarding his right flank, and the Qattara Depression his left. In the early morning of July 1 the armored strength of the opposing forces joined battle, and heavy fighting continued throughout the day. The Eighth Army repulsed repeated attacks by tanks and infantry, and on the evening of the 2nd the enemy retired, leaving the British positions intact. On the following day the British forces, with air support on a scale unprecedented on the Middle Eastern Front, counter-

EGYPT BEGINS

attacked, captured several hundred prisoners and put many enemy tanks out of action. This was followed on the 10th by an attack by British and South African troops, with tank and air support, who occupied the ridge of Tel el Eisa, after a five-mile advance. A similar attack was made from the south on the 15th by New Zealand and Indian infantry who succeeded in taking Ruweisat Ridge, south of El Alamein and advancing into the enemy positions seven miles. The pictures show: above; left, British tanks setting off at dawn to attack enemy positions, and right, Matildas, followed by men of the Scots Guards, going into action at El Alamein. The lower pictures show Bren carriers patrolling the forward areas of the battlefield.

German drive threatens Stalingrad and Rostov

FIGHTING IN THE DON BEND. Although the Germans had reached the very gates of Voronezh, they were unable to take it by storm. Farther south, however, a rapid advance along the railways brought about the fall of Kantemirovka (south of Rossosh) and of Lisichansk (100 miles southwest of Kantemirovka) on July 12, and heavy fighting was in progress near Boguchar which, together with Millerovsk, the Russians were obliged to evacuate on the 15th. This created a dangerous bulge in the Russian lines which threatened the industrial city of Stalingrad, on the Volga, and the port of Rostov at the mouth of the Don. The Russian

armies inside the Don bend fought fierce rearguard actions whilst retiring to their main defensive positions along the lower reaches of the river, but by the 16th fighting was taking place before Voroshilovgrad, and two days later the enemy was only seventy miles northwest of Rostov, and still advancing rapidly. On the following day Voroshilovgrad was evacuated by the Red Army in order to avoid encirclement. The pictures show: left, Russian sappers on the Voronezh sector crawling forward to clear a gap in a minefield for the passage of their tanks and infantry, and right, Soviet infantry equipped with automatic weapons.

CHARGING UNDER FIRE. Indian troops charge tnrough gaps in barbed wire (top), made with the aid of Bren gun carriers, as they advance to capture a stronghold in the desert, while below, men of an English regiment man their Vickers guns in a forward position as an enemy artillery shot finds the range close by. Men of all nations owing allegiance to the British Commonwealth played a part in the great campaign of the Eighth Army to oust the Axis from North Africa and eliminate the threat to Egypt, in which they wrote a glorious page in the annals of history during the dark days of the war for the United Nations.

SUCCESS IN NEW GUINEA. During the long campaign in Papua, New Guinea, the Australian troops played a part of conspicuous gallantry. Here three Aussies are seen in action in the jungle.

ADVANCE IN THE DESERT. Many daring and successful actions were fought by British troops during the fighting in the Libyan Desert. This picture shows British infantry charging through a smoke screen.

British hold the initiative in Egypt

GERMAN COUNTER-ATTACKS REPELLED. On July 16 German forces attempted to recapture the positions they had lost on Ruweisat Ridge, and a big tank battle developed in which twenty-five enemy tanks were destroyed. In the north, where enemy counter-attacks had regained part of the ground lost on Tel el Eisa, Imperial forces drove the enemy out of most of the lost positions. On the 21st General Auchinleck launched a general offensive all along the front, and fierce fighting raged throughout the night and the following day.

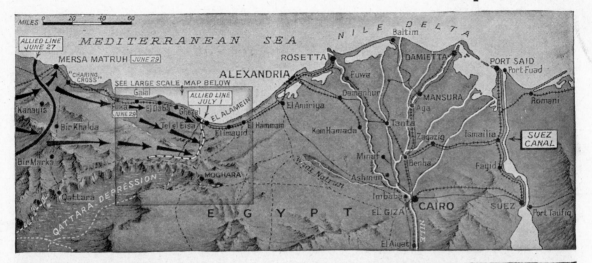

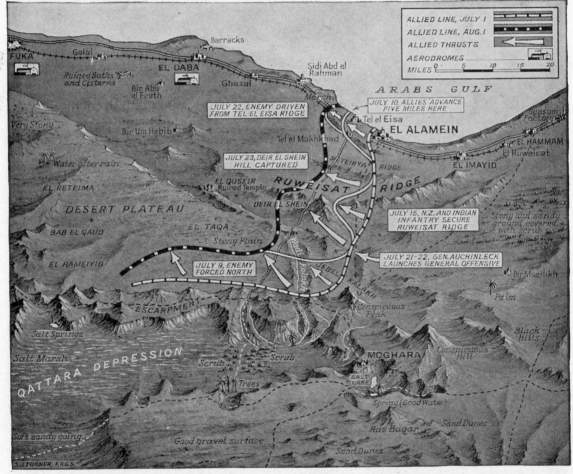

In this action South African troops drove the enemy from the whole of Tel el Eisa Ridge, while in the centre New Zealand infantry made considerable progress along Ruweisat Ridge. By the 25th fighting had died down, and the enemy began to "dig in." The pictures show: above, some of the Axis prisoners taken by the New Zealanders on Ruweisat Ridge, and below, loading up a General Grant tank ready for action. The maps show, above, the German advance (indicated by black arrows), and below, the main battle area.

719

A heavy British bomber prepares to scourge the Reich

FIRE BOMBS FOR GERMAN CITIES. During July the R.A.F. kept up its attacks on centres of German war production whenever weather permitted. Bremen, Wilhelmshaven, Danzig, Flensburg, Dusseldorf, Duisburg, Luebeck, Vegesack and Hamburg were visited, some of them more than once, and great material damage was done. Of these raids perhaps the most outstanding were the daylight raid on Danzig on the 11th and the night raid on Hamburg on the 26th. The former involved a flight of 1,750 miles—the longest

daylight operational flight yet attempted. In the Hamburg raid 175,000 incendiary bombs were rained on the city within fifty minutes—far surpassing the number dropped on London in the fire raid of December 29, 1940. Some idea of the weight of the British offensive may be gathered from the fact that during June and July, 1942, 13,000 tons of bombs were dropped on Germany as against 8,500 tons in the same months of 1941, and 3,500 in June and July, 1940. The Stirling bomber, seen above, is being loaded with incendiary bombs.

Germans recapture Rostov on the Don

FALL OF ROSTOV. After the evacuation of Voroshilovgrad, the German attack on Rostov was broadened by pressure both from Taganrog and Millerovo. On July 25, the enemy thrusts down the railways from Voroshilovgrad and Millerovo had linked up, and fighting on the whole Lower Don front became intense. Two bridges were thrown across the river at Tsymlyansk, and despite desperate Russian resistance, the railway joining Stalingrad with the Black Sea and the Caucasus was threatened. The superiority of the enemy in arms and numbers enabled him to consolidate his bridgehead and also to close in on Rostov.

After carrying out thorough demolitions, the great port was evacuated by the Russians on the 27th. On the same day another enemy threat to the Black Sea coast and the oil of Maikop took shape in a swift German drive south-eastwards to Bataisk. The pictures show: left, German infantry in Rostov crawling forward with the support of field guns; top, right, burnt-out street cars which had been used as barricades by the Russians during the desperate street fighing which raged in the town and suburbs before the final evacuation. The picture below, right, shows German infantry surrendering to the crew of a Soviet tank.

Germans open drive for the Caucasus oil fields

RUSSIAN OILFIELDS THREATENED. After the German capture of Rostov and Bataisk, fierce and prolonged fighting took place near Salsk and at Kuschev. Again the Soviet forces were driven gradually back, and on August 6, von Kleist's tanks, after crossing the Kuban river, entered Tikhoretsk. The Germans were now advancing on Maikop across the rich Kuban steppes, and on the 8th, they broke through towards Armavir and Krasnodar, thereby developing a dangerous pincers threat to Maikop. The pictures show: left, above, Red Army men attacking an enemy outpost in an attempt to stem the advance, and below, German troops occupying a railway station that has been "scorched" by the retreating Russians. Right, above, Germans advancing along a road choked with refugees. Below, Germans attacking a Building.

U.S. MARINES LAND IN THE SOLOMONS

AUGUST 7, 1942

In the early hours of August 7, warships and aircraft of the U.S. Pacific Fleet opened up a heavy bombardment on the Japanese positions in the Tulagi area of the Solomons, and U.S. marines went ashore in landing barges. By nightfall they had gained strong positions on Guadalcanal, Tulagi, and Florida, after having overcome fierce enemy resistance, and on the following day they extended the occupied area of Guadalcanal and captured a vital aerodrome. On Tulagi almost all resistance had been overcome and huge quantities of munitions and supplies had been captured. By noon on the 10th the marines were in firm control of Guadalcanal, Tulagi, Gavatu, Tanambogo, Makambo and Florida, and were engaged in mopping up enemy forces which had been defeated on the beachheads and had retreated to the interior. During these operations long-range U.S. bombers carried out extensive reconnaissance besides bombing enemy ships and air bases in New Britain, New Ireland, and in the Solomons area. The pictures show: unloading men and supplies on the island.

How Tulagi Island looked down a Navy bomb sight

BATTLE OF THE SOLOMONS. This is the famous Tulagi Island (center foreground), stronghold of the Japanese forces in the Solomon Islands. Fires can be seen burning (right center) after American carrier-based dive bombers paid their first visit with bombs. In addition to fortifications, anti-aircraft batteries and radio station the Japanese had a small golf course on the island, but the unexpected arrival of U.S. Navy bombers gave them no time to yell "FORE" to Tokio. The operation in the Solomons inaugurated a series of offensive moves in the Pacific which continued for several months. The enemy occupation of the Islands permitted him the use of advance air and naval bases from which to attack the allies long Pacific supply line and the north coast of Australia. On August 7, 1942, therefore, United States Navy and Marine forces seized beachheads on Guadalcanal and Florida Island and occupied Tulagi. The highly prized Henderson airfield on Guadalcanal was held by the Marines against a long series of heavy air, sea and ground assaults by the enemy. The resolute defense of these marines under Major General (now Lieutenant General) Alexander A. Vandegrift and the desperate gallantry of our naval task forces marked the turning point in the Pacific.

ENEMY STRONGHOLD BLASTED. Guns and planes of the Pacific fleet blast tiny Tanambogo Island, enemy stronghold in the Solomons, just prior to its capture by the Marines, on August 7. In the foreground is the famous causeway connecting with Gavut Island, which marines crossed under heavy machine gun fire. In the meantime, at Guadalcanal, the American transports engaged in unloading stores and equipment were attacked about midday by enemy planes, and shortly after midnight an enemy naval force, never clearly identified, appeared on the scene and managed to get between the outer defense task force, stationed near Savo Island and an inner guard lying close to the transports. Flares were dropped by

enemy planes on the south side of the Allied ships outlining these to the enemy, who promptly opened fire. In this sudden close-range exchange of fire the Australian cruiser Canberra was sunk, and also the American cruisers Quincy, Astoria and Vincennes. Loss to the enemy remains unknown, but he had failed to destroy or drive away the American transports and the marines were landed, and as shown in the picture above, proceeded to mop up the islands. His uniform and equipment painted to blend with the thick foliage, this Marine raider has just thrown a hand grenade and advances with a rush and a Reisling gun to clean up the machine gun nest before the enemy recovers from the shock.

Death on the battlefield and death by hari-kari

DEATH IN THE MORNING. The rising sun reveals the corpses of these Japanese jungle fighters, half buried in the tidal sands of the Tenaru River where they fell in their vicious night attempt to dislodge the U.S. Marines from Guadalcanal Island. Note the bullet hole in right eyebrow of the Japanese in foreground. These troops were part of the enemy reinforcements which arrived on Guadalcanal during the night of August 10-11 and came out second-best in hand to hand encounters with the United States Marines. The landings were made mostly at night and when American planes could not operate from Henderson Field, still in process of being constructed. The Japanese had started the building of Henderson Field but were interrupted by the American landings on Guadalcanal.

BATTLEFIELD. Bodies of Japanese who succeeded in crossing the mouth of the Tenaru during the action are shown strewn along the sands the day after the battle. Losses on both sides were extremely heavy.

THE JAPANESE WAY. Many Japanese preferred suicide to surrender which they believe is dishonorable. These two Japanese Marines placed the muzzle of their rifles against their foreheads and pushed the trigger with their toes. One of them (background) still has his toe on the trigger. In the early days of the South Pacific campaign the Japanese preferred death this way to surrender, but as the campaign progressed, more and more of the enemy allowed themselves to be taken prisoner.

RIOTING IN INDIA. After the failure of Sir Stafford Cripps' mission to India, the Congress Party, on July 10, issued a resolution demanding immediate British withdrawal. Shortly afterwards the Government of India raided Congress headquarters and seized the records of its proceedings. Among the documents confiscated was Gandhi's original draft resolution, submitted to the Working Committee on April 27, which contained a statement to the effect that if India were free one of her first steps would probably be to negotiate with Japan. The Government published the text of this draft on August 4, and on the following day Congress passed an amended resolution restating its demand for British withdrawal and threatening a mass civil disobedience campaign if its demands were not met. As a result the Government, on the 7th, issued an order forbidding the closing of shops dealing with vital necessities, and on the 9th arrested 148 Congress leaders, including Gandhi, Pandit Nehru, and Dr. Azad. Rioting broke out in Bombay and other cities and the police and military were called out to deal with the disturbances. Altogether 658 people were killed and 1,003 wounded by police and military action. Pictures show: above, the Yervada Palace, Poona, where Gandhi was imprisoned, and below, Gandhi in 1931.

THE TWAIN DOES MEET. Old and new ideas in transportation are seen as supplies for U.S. troops are carried along a highway in India, as the Americans joined their British allies to check the common foe.

American plane scores a bull's eye in the Pacific   August, 1942

A TRANSPORT GOES DOWN. A camouflaged Japanese transport sinking off New Britain after attack by a flying fortress. This was one of the many attacks on this important Japanese base by American bombers in an effort to stop the enemy from reinforcing his troops in the Bismarck Archipelago.

AL.. DRESSED UP. A close-up of the Japanese transport aflame in waters south of the Bismarck Archipelago. Note the intensive efforts to camouflage the ship with tropical foliage.

RUSSIAN OIL TOWN CAPTURED. After the German break through towards Armavir and Krasnodar, the defenders, on August 9, set the oilfields on fire and demolished all equipment. The Germans made unsuccessful attempts to blast out the fires by dropping demolition charges from planes near the blazing wells. On the 16th the town of Maikop had to be abandoned. The enemy also made rapid progress towards the Black Sea port of Novorossisk and along the northern side of the main Caucasus range. On the 10th they captured Piatigorsk, 120 miles south-east of Armavir, and four days later then entered Georgievsk, 120 miles north-west of the Grozny oilfields, on the Rostov-Baku railway. Meanwhile, in the Don bend, the Nazis continued to throw masses of men into the battle regardless of huge losses. On the 15th they succeeded in driving a wedge into the Russian positions at the Don elbow between Kletskaya and Kalach, forty miles north-west of Stalingrad. The pictures show: above, German troops captured by the Russians during the fighting in the North Caucasus, and left, Nazi soldiers passing some of the blazing oilfields near Maikop.

Pushing ahead through the jungles of New Guinea

HEAVY GOING. A group of American soldiers starts down a New Guinea road in single file to open a flanking movement against the Japanese. In the face of strong enemy resistance, American and

Australian troops continued their ever forward movement over mud-covered jungle roads to force the invaders back to the sea. A campaign that finally met with success despite the hardships involved.

CANADIANS LAND AT DIEPPE

AUGUST 19, 1942

The biggest combined operations carried out on the Continent since the evacuation of Dunkirk took place on August 19, when a large force, consisting mainly of Canadians, carried out a daring daylight landing at Dieppe and remained on French soil for nine hours before withdrawing. Officially described as a "reconnaissance in force," its objects were: (1) to test the defenses of what was known to be a strongly fortified part of the enemy coast; (2) the destruction of German batteries and an important radio-location station; and (3) the capture of prisoners for interrogation. Escorted by units of the British Navy, the force passed safely through the enemy minefields and landed according to schedule, at 4:50 a.m., on six selected beaches in the Dieppe area. At Varengeville, 4½ miles west of Dieppe, a Commando force succeeded in destroying an enemy 6-in. gun battery of howitzers, but at Berneval, 4½ miles east of Dieppe, a chance encounter with enemy E-boats and flak ships caused an inital set-back. Although landings were later made here, the enemy coastal guns were never silenced, and hindered the attackers on the central beaches throughout the operation. In the center, at Pourville and Puys, tanks were landed from special landing craft, and Canadian troops, with tanks in support, fought their way into the center of the town, where fierce fighting raged round the Casino. All the objectives of the raid were attained, and the withdrawal was carried out only six minutes after the scheduled time. All the tanks were blown up before re-embarkation. Throughout the day the Royal Navy supported the land operations by keeping up a constant bombardment of the enemy shore positions, and despite heavy retaliatory fire from German shore batteries only one ship, the destroyer Berkeley, was lost. Operational commands of the R.A.F., as well as Canadian, New Zealand, Polish, Czech, Belgian, Fighting French and Norwegian squadrons provided air cover for the attack, and Flying Fortresses of the U.S. Army Air Forces made a high-level raid on the airfield at Abbeville. The Germans called up air reinforcements from all parts of Occupied France, Belgium and Holland, but many of these were engaged and broken up by Allied airmen before they reached the scene of the operations. The picture shows British landing craft nearing Dieppe, despite a fierce barrage.

The Commandos approach the cliffs of Dieppe   August 19, 1942

BOUND FOR FRANCE. Quiet, relaxed, almost nonchalant, Canadian troops approach the cliffs of Dieppe for the most daring and complex Commando raid on highly fortified enemy positions.

THE NAVY'S PART. A naval motor launch seen with four of the landing craft during the operations. Despite the heavy fire from German shore batteries only one ship, H.M.S. Berkeley was lost.

FORTUNES OF WAR. Wounded soldiers being brought on board a British destroyer after raid on Dieppe. The wounded were evacuated from the town while the fighting continued, loaded on landing barges, they were convoyed to destroyers in the harbor while the R.A.F. put up an extensive air umbrella. While casualties were heavy fast work by medical detachments saved hundreds of lives.

Scenes in France and England after raid on Dieppe

SUCCESS OF THE DIEPPE RAID. Throughout the Dieppe raid an extensive air umbrella provided support for the ground forces, and during the day, air fighting developed on a scale not seen since the Battle of Britain. In spite of the fact that the Allied airmen were operating over enemy occupied territory, they shot down ninety-one enemy planes and damaged and probably destroyed twice that number. The Allies lost ninety-eight planes. The Germans tried to create the impression that the raid had been a full scale attempt at invasion, but this had been foreseen and forestalled by a B.B.C. broadcast to the French people during the

early stages of the operation, which urged them to avoid all action that would compromise their safety and told them that no invasion was contemplated. Canadians, who formed five-sixths of the attacking force, sustained casualties amounting to 3,350 men made up of 170 dead, 633 wounded, and 2,547 missing. The pictures show: left, above, a burning British landing craft and two Churchill tanks on the shore at Dieppe and below, a close-up view of a British tank whose tractor has been torn off. Some of the British airmen who took part in the operation are seen above, right, and below, other raiders at a British port.

CAUGHT ON THE GROUND. Here's one Japanese Zero that never got off the ground in the fight for Tulagi, one of the Japanese-held islands in the Solomons. It lies in a revetment, smashed by attacks of the U.S. Army Air Forces. Soldiers are repairing damage done by U.S. bombs and shells prior to the occupation of the island on the morning of August 7. The landings at Guadalcanal, two hours later, were preceded by a preliminary naval bombardment which drove the Japanese to take shelter in the limestone caves which honeycomb the region. At first little opposition was encountered at Tulagi, but when darkness fell the Japanese counter-attacked, emerging from the caves and from the jungles and considerable hand-to-hand fighting resulted in the darkness, but by next morning the Americans succeeded in clearing up the area.

CANINE MARINE. This German Shepherd dog stands by his master on the shores of a Pacific Island. Any foreign movement will be heard or spotted by him as he helps his master see that "the situation is well in hand." The landings in the Solomons marked the first time that a trained dog unit had been used by the American armed forces. The dogs were constantly employed during the operations of securing and extending the beachhead and proved themselves as messengers, scouts and agents of night security. In the field the dogs did very well on the C rations that were fed to the men. According to their trainers the dogs did even the marines credit, a great tribute from the "devil dogs," excellent fighters themselves. The dogs had been recruited from civilians in the United States and trained at various posts in America and Hawaii.

JEEPS AND MARINES. Jeeps, crowded with marines, push through the jungle on the Guadalcanal front.

MESSAGE FOR THE JAPANESE. An 80 mm mortar section in action during the fighting on Guadalcanal.

A long way from the Halls of Montezuma

IN THE SOUTH PACIFIC. A group of Marine Corps raiders on the move in full battle dress on one of the islands in the South Pacific as the campaign in the Solomons started to roll.

FRONT LINE DRESSING STATION. Men of the Navy's medical corps attending wounded marines brought to this front line dressing station on the Solomons by jeeps doubling as ambulances.

A PACIFIC ATOLL INVADED. A column of U.S. troops are photographed by a Coast Guard combat cameraman as they advance to continue the attack on the Japanese, who had been pushed back to the other end of this South Pacific atoll. A large Japanese seaplane is partially submerged in the lagoon following strafing by American planes. In the right foreground Japanese fuel barrels can be seen.

PRISONERS OF THE UNITED STATES. A group of Japanese prisoners of war being marched off to a prisoner of war camp on Guadalcanal, there to be treated with full honors of war in contrast to the treatment accorded Americans and British seized by the Japanese in the engagements in the South Pacific, details of which were revealed to a horrified world by Allied prisoners who were fortunate enough to escape.

FIGHTING IN THE DON ELBOW. On August 18 the German armies driving towards Stalingrad from the north-west reached the Don south-east of Kletskaya, and five days later they succeeded in getting tanks and men across on to the east bank under cover of an aerial umbrella. Farther south, the enemy drove a deep wedge into the Russian lines north-east of Kotelnikovo on the 24th thereby threatening Stalingrad from north and south. The pictures show: above, Cossack cavalry charging to attack the enemy during the fighting on the Don, and below, an aerial view of the Don elbow showing two out of three bridges destroyed.

CHURCHILL TALKS WI.H STALIN AND SMUTS. On August 17 it was announced that important conversations had taken place in Moscow between Winston Churchill, W. Averill Harriman and Marshal Stalin and that a number of decisions had been reached concerning the conduct of the war against Germany. On his return journey the British Prime Minister visited the Middle East where he conferred with Allied leaders and visited Allied troops on the desert battle front. During his stay he met General Smuts, prime minister of South Africa. In the top picture Mr. Churchill is shown in Moscow with Harriman, Stalin and Molotov.

The Duke of Kent dies in line of duty

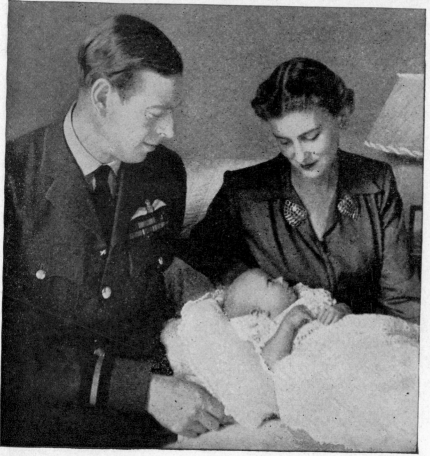

ROYAL TRAGEDY. On August 25 a Sunderland flying boat, carrying H.R.H. the Duke of Kent to Iceland, crashed on a lonely mountainside in Scotland, and all the occupants, except the rear-gunner, were killed. Born on December 20, 1902, the Duke married Princess Marina of Greece in 1934, by whom he had three children. The youngest, Prince Michael, was born on July 4, only a few weeks before his father's tragic death. The funeral took place at St. George's Chapel, Windsor, on August 29. The photograph, left, by Cecil Beaton, shows the Duke and Duchess with their youngest child; above, the Duke's coffin, draped with his personal standard, is seen on its arrival in London from Scotland.

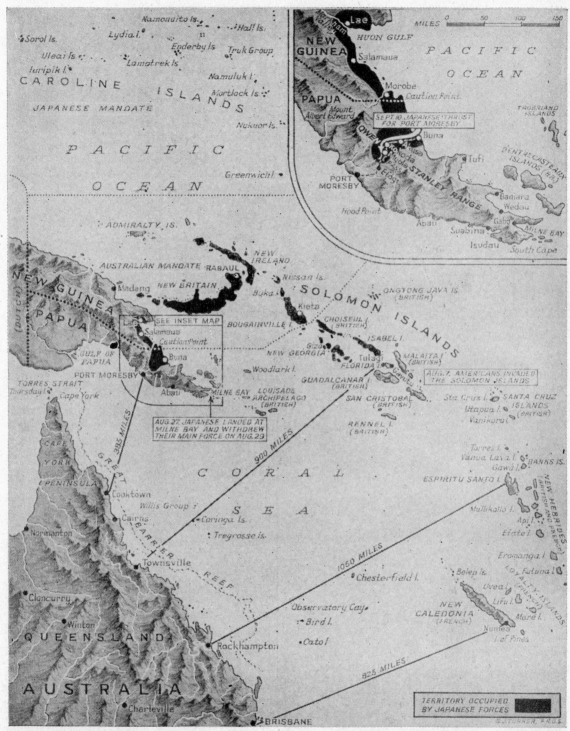

NEW LANDING IN PAPUA. In an effort to by-pass the Owen Stanley Mountains and capture Port Moresby, as well as to obtain an advance base for the recapture of their lost positions in the Solomons, Japanese troops landed at Milne Bay, Papua, on August 27. Allied aircraft and Australian troops were waiting, unknown to the enemy, and inflicted such severe losses on his forces that the bulk of them were withdrawn on the 29th. The map shows the main centers of fighting in this area of New Guinea.

Marine raiders establish a beach head in the Solomons

LANDING OPERATION. A true Marine Corps landing operation takes place on the tip of Guadalcanal Island as these soldiers of the sea come ashore from their landing craft during the preliminary fight to establish a beachhead on this South Pacific Island. These marines were part of a Raider battalion which was used with great success in landing operations in the South Pacific campaign. An expeditionary force of United States Marines, provided with a protective convoy and a task force arrived off the islands on August 6, and at dawn on August 7, split into two portions. One proceeded to the vicinity of Tulagi and the second to Guadalcanal. The approach to the area of operation was fortunately under cover of an overcast sky that made enemy aerial reconnaissance difficult. But on the night of August 6-7, the weather cleared. However, the expeditionary forces with their supporting craft proceeded to their assigned positions undetected, and the Japanese were taken by surprise. By nightfall on August 9 unloading operations had been completed and cargo ships left the area. By noon of August 10, they were fully involved and consolidated their positions on the islands of Guadalcanal, Tulagi, Gavutu, Tanamboga, Makambo and portions of Florida island

THE BATTLE FOR STALINGRAD OPENS

August 24, 1942

After throwing large infantry and tank forces across the Don on August 22-23 the Germans massed in strength for the final assault against Stalingrad. The enemy's terrific blows on land and from the air pressed the Russians back relentlessly towards the Volga. Plainly, they were prepared to throw in everything in order to seize this large and important industrial center —the key to the whole Russian defensive system. Von Bock's initial thrust for Stalingrad from the north-west, begun on August 24, was supported by masses of tanks and heavy artillery and hundreds of dive bombers. For days and nights battles raged with unparalleled ferocity at the city's approaches and appalling casualties were suffered by both sides. In determined counter-attacks on September 2-7, the Red Army threw the invaders back, though not before the outer defense ring had been penetrated deeply at many points. By September 12, 13 German tanks and artillery, as well as large infantry forces, had entered the suburbs and industrial areas of Stalingrad. Fierce hand-to-hand fighting raged among houses and factory buildings in the northern part of the city. At times, a floor of a building would be held by one side while the other held the floor below. So stubborn was the Russian resistance that the enemy, despite greatly superior numbers, advanced only by the yard and at bitter cost. Attack after attack was repulsed with heavy casualties to the Germans, and by October 12 all their infantry and tank thrusts had been temporarily halted. Meanwhile, Stalingrad was subjected to the heaviest mass air attacks of the war. Three-quarters of the city was smashed by the Luftwaffe. Defenses were breached, buildings razed, civilians murdered in thousands; smoke and dust enveloped the whole of Stalingrad in a permanent cloud. Yet the spirit of the defenders was unbroken. Fierce German attempts to break through to the Volga were launched again in late October and, after regrouping his forces a second time, von Bock made his final bid to win Stalingrad on November 12. It failed. The tide had turned, and on November 19 the Red Army started its offensive north and south of the city. A week later both forces joined up. Stalingrad was relieved after the terrible three-months' siege. Seventy thousand prisoners and vast booty fell to the Russian troops. This picture shows women crossing a devastated square on their way out of Stalingrad after the evacuation had been ordered.

Advancing Germans smash into the suburbs of Stalingrad

BITTER DEFENSE OF STALINGRAD CONTINUES. In their desperate and unavailing attempts to capture the city, the Germans were thwarted time and again by the demolition tactics employed by the Russians, who did not hesitate to destroy storehouses, war factories, and armament works rather than yield their possession to the enemy. The history of warfare shows no more stubborn defense than that of Stalingrad. The pictures show: above, German transport approaching the Stalingrad battle area; top, right, enemy artillery advance into the shambles of a suburb; bottom, right. Nazi soldiers find a former factory in ruins.

HOME DEFENSE WORK. Firemen battle a vicious blaze which was set during a German air raid on the British capital. The fire services brought the blaze under control after a stubborn battle. The work of these volunteers was of great help to the military during the raids on London.

AFTERMATH OF THE BLITZ. The unsafe walls of a bombed building in Central London is pulled down to clear the site for post war rebuilding. Thruout the city, damage caused by the many Nazi raids was rapidly cleared and the work of preparing for the post-war era went on despite continuance of Nazi raids.

BRAVE YUGOSLAV PATRIOTS DEFY THE INVADER

Ever since the German and Italian armies marched into Yugoslavia on April 6, 1941, the brave bands of native guerrillas in the mountains, forests and elsewhere continued their determined resistance against the hated invaders. In spite of repeated threats of shooting or torture in Nazi concentration camps, the patriots never for a single day ceased their activities of sabotage and train-wrecking as well as open armed combat. In the latter part of the summer of 1942 the whole railway system of Yugoslavia was brought to a complete standstill for about ten days because of widespread destruction done to tracks and rolling stock by the guerrillas. This brought about some considerable delay in the passage of German munitions and supplies which were being rushed through the Balkans to Rommel's harassed armies on the North African front. Many towns and villages throughout Yugoslavia were bombed from the air or burned to the ground by gangs of infuriated young Nazis, but the remarkable resistance of the patriot forces continued seriously to upset the enemy's plans. This resistance much increased when the guerrillas were properly organized into groups under various brave guerrilla leaders. On September 1 about 20,000 German and Croat Fascist troops began an offensive against the guerrillas in a rugged part of the Bosnian mountains, near the little town of Banjalucka. After fifteen days of fierce fighting the enemy were beaten back at all points, leaving the patriot forces in control of the whole area. In a surprise counter-offensive, detachments of the Yugoslav Army attacked enemy garrisons, took 200 prisoners and wiped out several Croat detachments who were forcibly taking grain and crops from the peasants. The picture shows the Nazis rounding up innocent women and children in a village of the Bosnian hills. These were but a few of the hundreds of peasants carried away to concentration camps as a reprisal for patriot defiance.

RENEWED FIGHTING IN EGYPT. On August 31 the Afrika Korps launched an attack on the British positions near Mt. Hemeimat. They were immediately engaged, and British bombers subjected them to a withering non-stop air attack. Although the enemy penetrated the British minefields at a few points, he was unable to pierce the defenses, and on September 2 he retired nine miles. The pictures show: above, a U.S. built tank travelling at speed near Mt. Hemeimat; below, a patrol dodging fire near Mt. Hemeimat.

GERMAN ADVANCE IN RUSSIA. After their advance near Kotelnikovo on August 24, both sides threw large numbers of reserves into the battle and fighting on a large scale developed along the whole front before Stalingrad. The Russians ceaselessly battered at the deep wedges the enemy had driven into their lines north and south of the city, but although they inflicted enormous losses on the enemy they were unable to halt them. The map shows the position on the Russian fronts as the third year ended.

THE FOURTH YEAR

SINCE July, 1942, the British Eighth Army and Rommel's Afrika Korps had been quiescent on the El Alemein line. On October 23 the British, now commanded by General Sir Bernard L. Montgomery, unleashed the great drive that was to write finis to Axis hopes for domination of North Africa and the conquest of Egypt. Bolstered by troop reinforcements, new American tanks and a protective aircraft umbrella, the British began a ten-day pounding of the Nazi emplacements that resulted in a break-through on November 3. By November 7 Rommel was in full retreat 240 miles west of El Alemein, pushing westward at a rate that had the British hard pressed to keep within striking distance of him. Tobruk fell November 13, then Bengasi November 21.

In mid-January, 1943, the Eighth Army was within 100 miles of Tripoli where the Afrika Korps was expected to make a stand. But, on January 24, Rommel gave up Tripoli and led his weary troops into Tunisia where he took temporary sanctuary behind the Mareth Line. In fifteen weeks Montgomery's men had performed the phenomenal military feat of advancing more than 1,500 miles.

NORTH AFRICAN LANDINGS

ALLIED strategy in North Africa became apparent on November 8, 1942, when a convoy of 850 Allied warships and troop transports arrived at several ports in Morocco and Algeria. American soldiers, in their first big operation in the European theatre, swarmed ashore at Casablanca, Oran and Algiers.

A successful political conquest had paved the way for the invasion, the initial objectives of which were accomplished with little bloodshed. Algiers fell by nightfall of the first day, Oran on November 10, and Casablanca a day later. Admiral Jean Darlan, the former Axis collaborator, then ordered an end to resistance and all Morocco and Algeria passed under Allied control.

The plan of battle that then became evident was to strike at the Axis' western flank while Montgomery was pressing them from the East. From Sicily the Germans began pouring heavy reinforcements into Tunisia where it became obvious that they would make their last stand in North Africa. American and British troops began driving into Tunisia a few days after the initial landings.

DEVELOPMENTS IN FRANCE

IN France, Hitler's response to the North African landings was an immediate occupation of the entire country with the single exception of the Toulon area. The bulk of the French navy was anchored in Toulon and Hitler's discretion was interpreted as an invitation to the fleet commanders to turn over their vessels to the Reich. On November 27, apparently impatient of the French failure to cooperate, Hitler ordered Toulon taken and the fleet seized. The French officers promptly scuttled about 60 ships, and a few that were still seaworthy escaped to join the Allies.

STALINGRAD

THE Russian theatre was being dominated by the exhaustive efforts of the Nazis to take Stalingrad and the heroic Russian defense of that city. By September 1, 1942, Stalingrad was under siege, German troops having established a foothold on the west bank of the Volga river. In a few weeks they were within the city, engaged in street to street fighting with Russian forces. In early October the German High Command virtually admitted the failure of their assault by announcing that it would depend on heavy artillery to level the city. By the end of the month the Red Army had started a counter-move against the rapidly tiring enemy. Picked units gradually encircled Stalingrad in preparation for the drive which later cut off the German army.

On November 22 the big Russian offensive was under way on three sectors of the long front. From Rezhev, a drive was made towards Velikie Luki, and, from Voronezh, another spearhead was directed at Kharkov. In the Stalingrad area a flanking movement was begun which, by January 10, 1943, had cut off the retreat of 330,000 Nazis and placed them under siege within the city. On February 2 the Soviet Command announced the surrender of the German garrison and the end to one of the bloodiest battles in history.

A few hundred miles south, the Russians were mopping up the Germans in the Caucasus area. During the summer of 1942 the invaders had penetrated as far as Nalchik and

Georgievsk. The Russians recaptured Georgievsk on January 11 and then pressed towards the Sea of Azov. By February 8, the Red Army had taken most of the key cities on this body of water and were closing in on Rostov.

GUADALCANAL

SINCE August 7, 1942, American Marines had been struggling to maintain their grip on the tropical jungles of Guadalcanal. While of a minor character from the standpoint of the numbers involved, the battle for the Solomons was important in that the safety of Allied supply lines to Australia were at stake. Also, an American victory was necessary to insure the success of further operations against the Japanese Pacific outposts.

The fate of the Solomons campaign was really decided in two major naval battles which were fought off Guadalcanal on the nights of November 12-13 and November 14-15. In these two engagements the Japanese lost 28 warships and transports, a price which discouraged them from any further large-scale attempts to regain control of Guadalcanal. For months the Japanese maintained small garrisons on Guadalcanal and other islands of the Solomon group, but American control of the seas blocked their supply lines and brought about their eventual defeat.

From Buna, on the northeast coast of New Guinea, which the Japanese had taken early that year, the enemy began a drive towards Port Moresby on September 9, 1942. This was the beginning of a bitter campaign for the control of the island. The Japanese were finally stopped at the Owen Stanley mountain range by Americans and Australians under General Douglas MacArthur. As Allied air strength increased, the Japanese were pushed back to their bases on the Bismarck Sea.

VICTORY IN TUNISIA

DURING the winter of 1943 Allied progress in Tunisia was at a standstill. Axis reinforcements from Sicily and a muddy terrain contributed equally to the stalemate. But in mid-April the British Eighth Army struck in the south and American and British First Army forces advanced in the North and West. Simultaneously, on May 7, American troops captured Bizerte and the British took Tunis. The conquest of this area left open only the Cape Bon Peninsula into which the Eighth Army drove the remaining German and Italian troops. On May 12 all resistance in Tunisia had ended, and the Allies held 252,415 prisoners and a large amount of equipment.

The Tunisian campaign was followed by the conquest of Sicily, on the south coast of which the initial American and British beachheads were established on July 10. The invading force was composed of the American Seventh Army and the battle-hardened British Eighth. The Americans moved north and west while the British veterans drove up the east coast. The capital of Palermo was taken on July 23 by the Americans who then turned east in the direction of Messina. Moving slowly against heavier opposition, the British took Catania on August 5 and drove the Axis towards Messina, the evacuation point to the mainland. When the Seventh Army took Messina on August 17, the Sicilian campaign was over.

THE ALEUTIANS

THE summer of 1943 was marked by the American recapture of two of the principal Aleutian islands which the Japanese had taken in 1942. A strong American naval task force protected the landing of troops on Attu on May 11. After a minor but bloody campaign, Washington announced on May 30 the end of Japanese resistance. On August 15 a well balanced U. S. fleet arrived off Kiska only to find the island deserted of Japanese.

After the Stalingrad disaster, the German High Command had resorted to defensive warfare. Throughout the long spring little ground was exchanged by either the Red Army or the Nazis. On July 5 the Germans launched the abortive offensive in the Kursk area, but two weeks later the Russians were pounding them back and took Orel on August 5. Their big summer success was the recapture of Kharkov on August 23.

AIR OFFENSIVE

AT the end of the fourth year, the Axis was on the defensive on all fronts. In addition to the pressure on the Russian, Mediterranean and Pacific areas, German's key cities were being subjected to a terrific round-the-clock bombing by British and American planes from English bases. Allied strategists were confident that this continual hammering, with its toll of German production, would provide an adequate temporary substitute for the western front action demanded by Russia.

SUPREME COMMANDER. General Dwight D. Eisenhower, Supreme commander in chief of Allied Forces, photographed at his headquarters in North Africa, in front of the British and American national emblems and the four-star flag of a general of the United States Army. Fresh from his success in the African and Mediterranean theatres, this picture of General Eisenhower was taken shortly before his promotion to supreme allied commander-in-chief and before he transferred his headquarters to London, from which point he took over the preliminary task of preparing for the invasion of the continent, which was scheduled to come in the spring or early summer of 1944.

The fourth year opens with all eyes on Stalingrad

FACTORY WORKERS SHOOT AT RAIDERS. As the fighting for Stalingrad reached a terrific climax, the defenders turned every house into a fortified point and every factory into a fortress. When the Germans began their massed air attacks early in September, workers throughout the city formed themselves into auxiliary anti-aircraft units. On September 4, forty-nine enemy bombers out of a force of 150 were shot down during a single raid. Picture shows members of a workers' battalion firing at German planes.

RED ARMY COUNTER-ATTACKS NEAR STALINGRAD. On September 4, the Red Army launched a surprise counter-attack to the south-west of Stalingrad where the enemy had driven deeply into the city's main defenses. In close-range fighting which lasted many hours, eleven German tanks were destroyed and 600 of the enemy killed. On the same day, to the north-west of the city, the Russians repulsed strong tank attacks with heavy enemy losses. This dramatic picture shows Red Army infantry advancing.

Heroic Russian resistance in devastating air raids

STALINGRAD WOMEN ENDURE WORST AERIAL BOMBARDMENT.

The weeks of heavy air raids on Stalingrad, which preceded the street fighting, were the most severe experienced by any civil population up to that time. Yet while buildings were falling overhead, women in cellars and caves far below the streets were busily occupied on vital work. Here they filled shells and hand grenades for the Red Army soldiers who were feverishly stemming the enemy's advance. Only between the bombings were they able to crawl up into the open in order to get food and water and wood for fuel. Above ground, the nurses of the city carried on calmly, going from one Red Army defense post to another. The pictures show: left, Nazi soldiers watching a Stalingrad woman emerge from a cellar; top, right, women searching for belongings after an air raid; bottom, right, women come up after a raid.

The Yanks and the Aussies advance in New Guinea

MARCHING ALONG TOGETHER. After the failure of the Japanese landing at Milne Bay, Papua, on August 27, the enemy made an unsuccessful thrust for Port Moresby on September 10. The Australians began their advance into the Owen Stanley mountains on September 28, and recaptured Myola and Kagi

without opposition on October 4. While Allied troops penetrated the Kokoda Gap on the Buna side before making contact with the enemy, their progress was hampered by the often impassable jungle and torrential rains. Above, Australian and American soldiers are shown building a road through the deep jungle.

New Guinea jungle conquered by Yanks and Aussies

CROSSING NEW GUINEA JUNGLE

Behind the news of the Allied progress through the dense and almost trackless jungle of New Guinea lay the splendid work of Australian and U.S. engineers. They performed remarkable feats of road and bridge building under the most difficult conditions. These pictures show: top, left, Australian engineers building a suspension bridge over a wild jungle stream; top, right, bridging operations near Kokoda in the Owen Stanley range; below, American soldiers wading through a swollen river.

WAR IN THE JUNGLE. On the world's toughest battlefront, Australian and American Forces maintained progress in the New Guinea jungle throughout September and October. By October 28, the Australians had overcome determined Japanese resistance in the Alola area, just south of Kokoda. After five weeks fighting, Kokoda was retaken on November 2. Thus the enemy lost their last foothold on the Buna side of the Owen Stanley Mountains. The Australians proved superb jungle fighters in a country of almost trackless bush, where natives acted as carriers for supplies. Natives are seen crossing a jungle torrent.

BATTLE OF THE SOLOMONS. The reconquest of the Solomons by U.S. Marines, which began on August 7, involved hard fighting. Fierce resistance was encountered on Guadalcanal, where the trapped Japanese Forces fought to the last man. On September 3, Marines attacked enemy landing-parties in the south-east of the group, and U.S. bombers scored hits on several ships. On September 9-12, strong Japanese air formations raided Tulagi and Guadalcanal, destroying twenty Allied planes. Despite these air attacks the Marines strengthened their positions. Above, an American patrol carrying wounded back to a jungle base.

Yankee surprise for the Japanese on New Guinea

LANDING OF PARATROOPERS. A view of a paratroop landing back of the foe's lines on New Guinea. Below and to the right of the leading plane may be seen several parachutes in various stages of opening.

swinging men at extreme angles and very close to the ground. The paratroopers, with their surprise tactics, played an important part in the retaking of New Guinea soil from the Japanese invaders.

The aircraft carrier Wasp goes down in the Coral Sea

SINKING OF THE WASP. On September 15, the 14,700-ton U.S. aircraft-carrier Wasp was attacked and sunk by a Japanese submarine in the Coral Sea, although its loss was not announced officially until October 26. At the time the ship was escorting a large supply convoy bound for Guadalcanal in the Solomon Islands which, however, reached port safely. Soon after the aircraft-carrier had been hit by three of the enemy torpedoes, she went down in an inferno of flame and smoke. Ninety per cent of the ship's crew managed

to get away in time, and were later picked up by escort vessels of the U.S. Navy. This remarkable picture, taken from the deck of one of the ships in the convoy, shows dense clouds of smoke billowing from the abandoned aircraft-carrier just before she went down. The Wasp, which was launched in 1939, had a proud record of war service. She earned much renown earlier in the year for her ferrying of reinforcements to Malta, making many voyages through the hazardous part of the Mediterranean.

From the halls of Montezuma to the shores of Guadalcanal

ON TO GUADALCANAL. Looking from the air like a zig-zaging squadron of water bugs, troop-carrying barges carry U. S. Marine reinforcements to the beach of Florida Island during one of the stages of the battle for the Solomons. The Marines seized beachheads on both Florida and Guadalcanal and occupied Tulagi. Heavy Japanese opposition was encountered on Guadalcanal and during August and September the enemy, at night, continued to land small contingents of troops at distant spots at Guadalcanal. During all this period the Japanese were well aware that the American position was little more than a beachhead some six to seven miles long and three miles deep—the western boundary being the Matanikau River and the eastern boundary Henderson Field. However, early in October the marines started another offensive west across the Matanikau River which they succeeded in crossing, and also cleared out a Japanese bridgehead a few days later, but it was not until early in 1943 that the Japanese ended all opposition to the American occupation of the Solomons.

Leathernecks take time out enroute to the front

MOVING UP IN THE JUNGLE. A detachment of U.S. Marines pauses in a jungle clearing for a brief rest enroute to the front on Guadalcanal Island. The marine in the right foreground has attached to his helmet netting for use in camouflaging himself in the dense undergrowth. Shortly after this photograph was taken these leathernecks drove an enemy band far into the hills. Commenting on the campaign in the Solomons, Admiral Ernest J. King, commander in chief of the United States fleet on October 18, 1943, said: "Because the Japanese through the subsequent weeks and months were determined that Guadalcanal, with its Henderson field, should not be lost to them, the whole story of what the United States Marines did there is one which is too big, too involved, and too valiant to be reported in a summary as brief as this. But as the world knows by now the marines, in their victory at Guadalcanal, completed an ageless epic for American history."

SOUTH AFRICAN PREMIER VISITS BRITAIN. On October 14, Field Marshal Smuts arrived in Britain by air for important consultations with the War Cabinet. On October 21, the famous Imperial statesman and soldier received a great welcome from the members of both Houses of Parliament whom he addressed at Westminster. In the course of his speech he paid a warm tribute to the fortitude of the British people and the courage, foresight and energy of its leader, Winston Churchill. "The defense phase has now ended," he said. "The stage is set for the last, the offensive phase." In the picture above the Field-Marshal is seen delivering his address in the chamber. On the extreme left is the late Speaker of th House, Captain Fitzroy. To the right are Mr. Churchill and Viscount Simon. Lloyd George presided over the meeting.

WOMEN GATHER THE HARVEST. In a broadcast on October 11, R. S. Hudson, British Minister of Agriculture, announced that the 1942 harvest in England had been the greatest on record. Britain started the war having lost 3,000,000 acres of agricultural land by building and several hundred thousand more for new airdromes and factories. Nevertheless, the area under crops had increased by more than half since war began, and was, in fact, greater than in 1918. In the past summer thousands of women had played an important part on the land, tackling every kind of agricultural work. In this way men were released for other duties. The picture shows a Woman's Land Army team cutting wheat on a downland farm in south England. A few years ago this land was derelict, but the demands of war transformed the scene.

FAMINE VICTIMS IN CHINA

During October, 1942, a famine occurred in the province of Northern Honan which threatened about 20,000,000 people with starvation. This was brought about by nearly two years of severe drought and a plague of locusts, unparalleled for centuries, which ruined the grain and rice fields. The blighted area extended over more than 20,000 square miles, and the districts which suffered most acutely were along the Yellow River in the neighborhood of Cheng Chow, a town which lay only a dozen miles from the Japanese lines. While millions of people were able to leave the province for other parts of China, those who remained had to live on grass, straw, weeds and even the bark of trees. The disaster was greatly aggravated by Japanese troops who had for a long period been systematically burning fields, crops and villages in an attempt to put an end to the activities of the Chinese guerrilla bands. These gallant bands, in spite of many handicaps, had for long been a worry to the Japanese invaders. China was now in the sixth year of her war against Japan, and though she had lost much territory and had sacrificed countless lives, her armies still stood firm in the path of the aggressor. The spirit of the country was still a glorious example for the world. So this additional disaster of famine was borne as bravely as were all her other sufferings. China's plight, however, was a serious one, especially as the loss of the Burma Road supply route made it extremely difficult for America, Britain and other Allies to come to her aid. The picture shows one of the many thousands of poor victims of what was probably the worst famine in the recorded history of China.

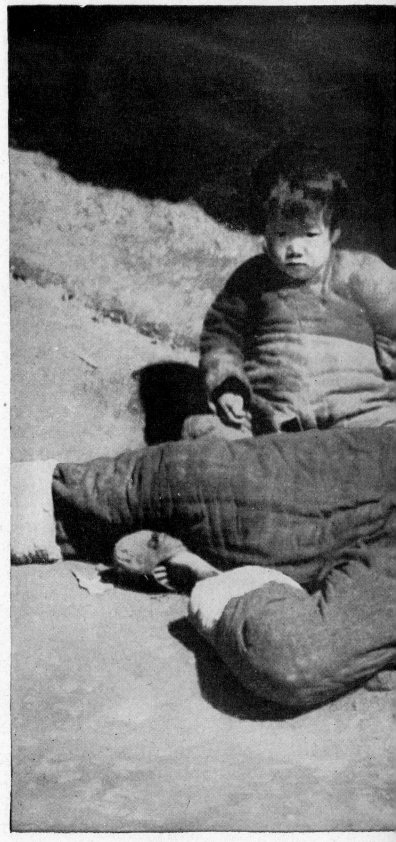

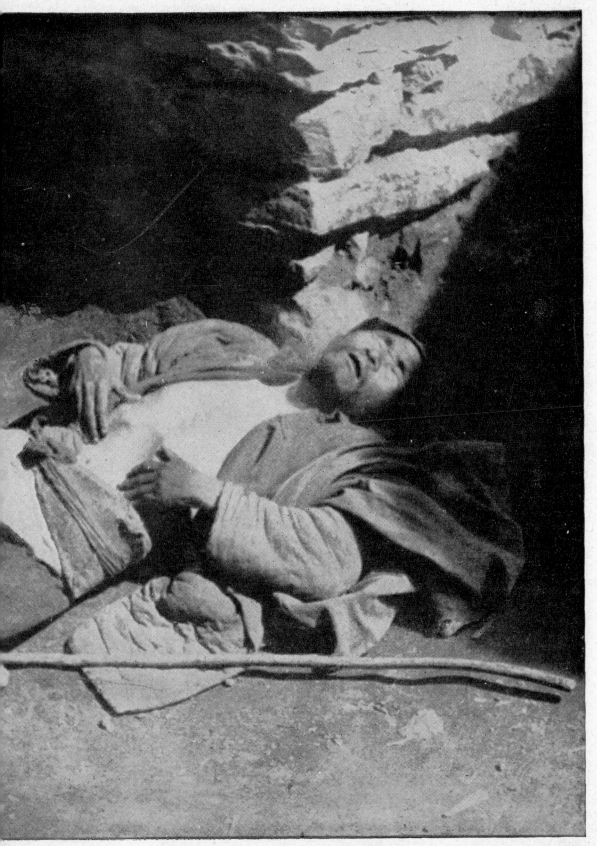

Carrying supplies to Russia over the Arctic route

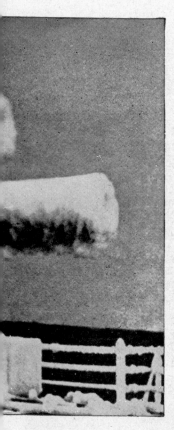

WINTER CONDITIONS ON THE ARCTIC CONVOY ROUTE. On October 6, the United States diplomatic representatives of Great Britain and the U.S.S.R. signed a protocol covering deliveries of military equipment and war material to Russia. The bulk of supplies had to be carried in convoys along the far northern route to Murmansk and Archangel, one of the most hazardous sea passages in the world. Apart from the menace of enemy submarines and shore-based aircraft, convoys had to fight their way through raging snow blizzards and seas infested with deadly ice floes, as the winter set in. These pictures of ice-coated decks on the ships of a Russia-bound convoy and escort give a vivid idea of the hardships endured.

Furious Nazi onslaught hurled back at Stalingrad

STREET FIGHTING IN STALINGRAD. On October 18 the Moscow radio declared that the decisive stage of the battle for Stalingrad had been reached. The enemy, using masses of infantry, tanks, artillery and air-craft, launched "all-out" attacks both in the northern factory area and in a southern thrust parallel to the Volga. But after bitter fighting, especially around the Red October and Red Barricade factories, they failed to gain any fresh ground and lost several thousand men and twenty-eight tanks. On October 23 German infantry detachments suffered heavy casualties in hand-to-hand fighting, and two enemy tanks which penetrated into the Red October works were destroyed. For several weeks the Germans made attack

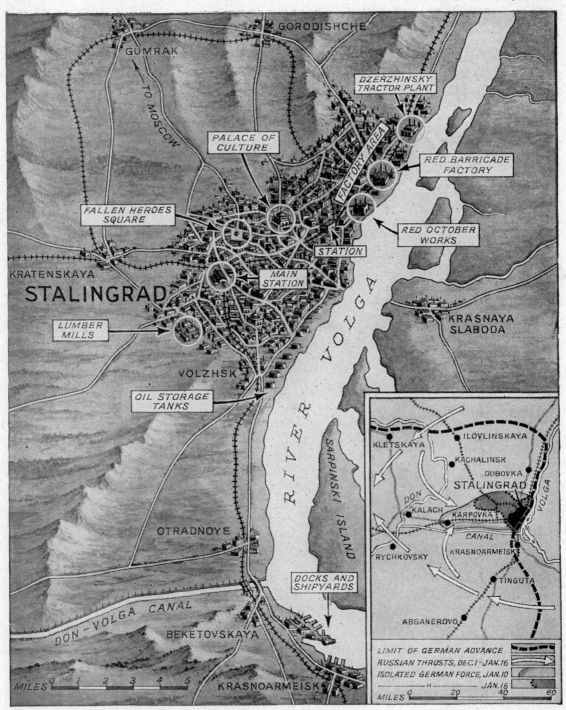

after attack in the northern factory area of Stalingrad, but every one of them was repulsed by the Red Army. The German casualties mounted steadily day by day. By November 8-10, the Russian defenders had regained or destroyed many blockhouses and factory buildings which had been enemy strong points a few days earlier, and what advances the enemy was now able to make were weak and ineffective. Russian tenacity was, at long last, to gain its well-deserved reward. Seldom, if ever, in history has a more bloody and prolonged hand-to-hand fight taken place. In the picture, left, Red Army riflemen are seen in action in a Stalingrad street. The map of Stalingrad, right, shows the farthest enemy advance into the city

R.A.F. STRIKES AT ITALY'S WAR INDUSTRY

On the night of October 22 a powerful force of British four-motored bombers flew 1,400 miles across the Alps and back to drop a great weight of bombs, including many 4,000-pounders, on the Italian port of Genoa. Nearly twenty major fires were started all over the city, and R.A.F. pilots saw oil storage tanks and munitions dumps in the dock area blown into the air by direct hits. Another heavy attack was made on the city the following night when targets at Turin and Savona were also bombed. This was only the beginning of a sustained air offensive against the chief ports and manufacturing cities in North Italy, where Mussolini's war industry was almost entirely concentrated. The bombing was part of the Allied plan to smash the Italian war machine and also to hamper the Axis forces in Libya and Tripolitania while the Eighth Army was making its great advance westwards. Genoa, besides having vital arms factories, power stations and dock installations, was the chief port of supply for Rommel's armies. On October 24 a force of more than eighty home-based Lancaster bombers made the first daring daylight raid on Milan, attacking their targets from such a low altitude that many of the R.A.F machines flew in below the level of the balloon barage over the city to release their loads of bombs. Nevertheless, in spite of much lively opposition from the anti-aircraft defenses, all except three of the British planes returned safely. The attack on Milan was continued after dark on the same day. For just as the Lancasters arrived back in Britain a stronger force of Stirlings, Wellingtons and Halifaxes took off from their bases to raid the Italian city again. On November 7 Genoa suffered its heaviest raid of the war so far when a great force of British bombers rained high explosive and incendiary bombs over a wide area of the city, leaving fires spreading rapidly among the warehouses and dock installations. Like many other cities in North Italy which were to feel the weight of R.A.F. blows in the weeks and months ahead, Genoa was obviously ill-prepared to meet these large-scale air attacks. The civil defense and fire-fighting organizations were thrown into such a state of confusion that they were quite unable to deal adequately with the many widespread fires and the dislocation of essential public services. The photograph shows loads of rubble collected from the devastated areas in Genoa being unloaded along the waterfront and dumped.

ANTI-U-BOAT WAR-FARE INCREASED

After the British First Lord of the Admiralty had announced in Parliament in September, that 530 U-boats had been sunk or damaged since outbreak of war, new and more deadly methods were taken against the enemy at sea in the following month, when successes in the Atlantic, the Mediterranean and elsewhere were much more encouraging. On November 1 the new Anti-U-boat Warfare Committee held its first weekly meeting in London to discuss new means of grappling with the peril at sea. This organization, marking a new phase in Allied sea warfare, was formed out of the Battle of the Atlantic Committee which had been set up by Winston Churchill in February, 1941. The pictures show: above, the crew of a damaged Italian submarine surrendering to a British destroyer in the Mediterranean; bottom, left, a German U-boat returning to its concrete "pen" inside the well-protected harbor at Lorient; bottom, right, the crew of another Italian submarine in the water awaiting their rescue by Allied ships.

BRITISH OFFENSIVE IN EGYPT BEGINS

The long-expected attack by the Eighth Army began in bright moonlight on the night of October 23 at El Alamein, following the heaviest gun barrage ever put up in the Western desert. For this preliminary softening of Rommel's deep defense lines the Allied artillery were ranged on a front of six miles with one gun to every twenty-three yards. For several hours a hell of fury was let loose on the enemy's positions before the Eighth Army, with powerful air, artillery and tank support, went forward to the attack. General Sir Bernard L. Montgomery used entirely new tactics in this battle by making a frontal attack against an unbroken line of trenches and minefields. The first stages of the attack were carried out by British and Dominion infantry, who, by dawn on October 24 had penetrated four miles through the gap in the enemy's advanced minefields. The enemy's main positions were successfully attacked at several points and many German and Italian prisoners were taken. Heavy fighting continued throughout the day and night while our troops consolidated their positions, and by the evening of October 25 the number of prisoners taken had mounted to 1,450. Meanwhile, the Allied Air Forces, working in perfect co-operation with the Eighth Army, kept up their non-stop blitz on enemy troop concentrations, landing-grounds, transport and supply lines. On the first day of the attack well over a thousand sorties were made by Allied bombers and fighters, dealing devastating blows on Rommel's communications and paving the way for the advance. On the night of November 1 General Montgomery launched a great offensive with strong tank support on a 4,000-yard front fifteen miles west of El Alamein. British infantry, fighting their way through minefields, barbed-wire and booby traps, had at last cleared a way for the armored forces. All day long on November 2 the great tank battle raged at El Aqqaqir. This was the turning-point which led to the clearing of the enemy from Egypt and their pursuit into Libya. The picture shows a long line of British tanks moving up to the front.

NAVY BRINGS SUPPLIES ASHORE. Right from the first day of General Montgomery's advance at El Alamein the British Navy maintained the closest co-operation with the British forces on land. Between October 24 and November 3 naval units, operating from Alexandra, carried out operations in the enemy's rear, shelling defenses along the coast. Although the ships were attacked from the air they suffered no losses. With the reoccupation of Sollum and Bardia on November 12 the Eighth Army had now won back several useful ports on the Mediterranean to which the Royal Navy could bring regular supplies. Fresh water was one of the major problems of warfare in this arid desert country, particularly on account of the speed of the British advance. But the Navy, true to its tradition, helped to provide a solution. Soon after British troops had entered Solum 33,000 barrels of water, each containing about 44 gallons, were brought ashore at Sollum by improvised landing craft. This picture shows some of the barrels being rolled onto the beach.

ROMMEL CHASED FROM EGYPT. On November 3 the Eighth Army began the pursuit of Rommel's battered divisions towards Libya. Next day the Africa Korps was in full flight, leaving behind 13,000 prisoners and vast quantities of material. By November 6 Axis prisoners totalled 20,000 and the British had captured some 400 tanks, 350 guns and thousands of vehicles. After slight resistance Mersa Matruh was regained on November 8 and Sidi Barrani on November 10. The coast road towards Sollum and the Halfaya Pass became choked by the retreating enemy, whose columns were thrown into hopeless confusion by the incessant strafing of Allied bombers. By November 10 the Eighth Army was established on both sides of Halfaya, a contingent of Dominion troops having moved up from the south. Large number of Axis troops were trapped between Halfaya and Sollum. On November 11 the Halfaya Pass was captured and over 1,100 prisoners, mainly Italians, fell into British hands. As the Axis forces retreated Italian engineers were detailed to blow up the coast road at Halfaya. It took great numbers of them four days and nights to finish the demolitions. Nevertheless, the Eighth Army's engineers (above) replaced it within twenty-four hours.

STILL SMILING. Captain Edward V. Rickenbacker, still smiling despite his ordeal, is shown in a jeep on a south Pacific island after his rescue from the sea 600 miles north of Samoa. Captain Rickenbacker had been lost since October 2 on a flight from Hawaii. Discovered on the life raft with Captain Rickenbacker were: Captain William T. Cherry, jr., pilot of the plane; Colonel Hans C. Adamson and Private John F. Bartek. One member of the crew, Alexander Kaczmarczyk, died on the raft and was buried at sea. Three other members of the party were found on a small island and returned safely to America.

BOUND FOR DAVEY JONES LOCKER. Plunging bow first to the bottom of the Pacific, a medium sized Japanese cargo ship is seen through the periscope of the submarine, USS Wahoo. The Wahoo sank the ship during a patrol in which she accounted for a total of eight Japanese vessels. The submarine has since been reported "overdue and presumed lost" on a South Pacific mission against enemy shipping.

Eighth army pursues the "desert fox" to Benghazi

LIBYAN PUSH GOES ON

On November 13 South African troops under General Pienaar occupied Tobruk and freed hundreds of native soldiers who had been in German hands there for five months. Thus was avenged the loss of the 2nd South African division at Tobruk in Rommel's offensive of the previous summer. By the next day the Eighth Army had advanced to Tmimi, sixty miles beyond Tobruk, where the retreating enemy, heavily bombed and strafed by the Allied air forces, was unable to put up any delaying rearguard action. On November 15 the finest airfield in the Western desert fell into British hands by the capture of Maturba. During the next few days operations were slowed down by bad weather. Nevertheless, General Montgomery's forces made progress to the north and south of Benghazi. One of the R.A.F.'s heaviest attacks in the Western desert was made on the docks at Benghazi before its occupation by British and Dominion troops on November 20. During the attack seven Ju 52s were shot down and many destroyed on the ground, while two ships were left burning. The pictures show: top, left, a British Bren carrier negotiating enemy barbed wire, and, top, right, a German tank crew surrendering to British infantrymen. Below is a remarkable picture of a desert sandstorm, one of many with which the Eighth Army had to contend during its advance.

Route of the British drive from Benghazi into Tripolitania

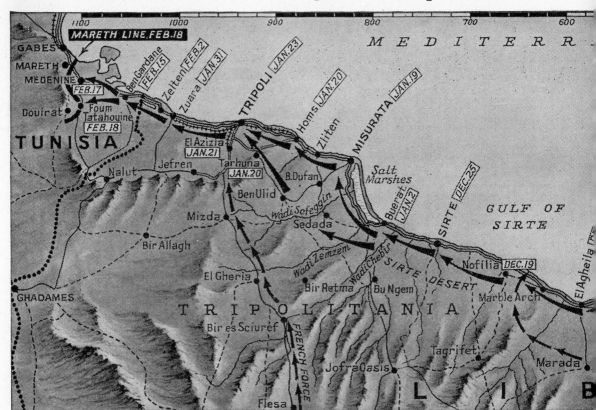

BATTLE FOR EL AGHEILA. After the recapture of Benghazi on November 20 the Eighth Army continued to pursue the Axis forces relentlessly towards El Agheila. Bad weather made the going very hard and the loosened sand after heavy rains seriously hindered the progress of British tanks and supply vehicles. These unfavorable conditions also restricted air activity for some days. Nevertheless, forward units of the Eighth Army maintained contact with the enemy's rearguards in the area around Jedabia, and this place was occupied by British troops on November 23. Air operations were resumed on November 26 when a strong bomber force attacked the Axis landing ground at "Marble Arch" and started large fires among

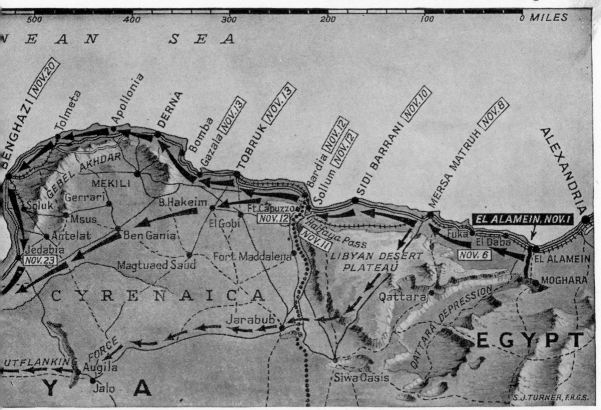

hangars and dispersed aircraft. During the lull in the land fighting, General Montgomery concentrated his troops near El Agheila, where Rommel was expected to make a last stand before Tripoli. On December 13 the Eighth Army attacked in strength and occupied Rommel's main defenses at Mersa Brega, east of El Agheila. Although El Agheila itself offered very good natural defenses, the Africa Korps had begun its retreat westwards again even before the Eighth Army delivered the main attack. The map above shows details of the British advance from El Alamein to El Agheila, which was taken on December 13, and the subsequent victorious drive to Tripoli. The pictures below show the difficult conditions for transport action.

AMERICANS LAND IN FRENCH NORTH AFRICA

Early on November 8, a few hours after the first parties of the American Expeditionary Force had been put ashore at many points on the coasts of Algeria and Morocco, the world heard the news of the greatest combined military operation in history. In the statement issued from Allied headquarters it was revealed that the entire operations were under the supreme command of Lieutenant-General Dwight D. Eisenhower of the United States Army and were supported by powerful units of the Royal Navy and Allied Air Forces. Steps were taken immediately to inform the French people, by radio and leaflets, of the landings and to assure them that the Allies sought no territory and had no intention of interfering with the French authorities in Africa. The landings were designed to forestall the occupation by the Axis powers of any part of North or West Africa, and to deny to the enemy a starting point from which a possible attack might be launched against the Atlantic seaboard of the Americas and the British West Indies. They also provided an effective second front for relieving the great pressure on the Russians and, moreover, were the first bold step towards the liberation of France and her Empire. Another important factor was the timing of the landings in French North Africa to coincide with the Eighth Army's offensive against Rommel in the Western desert. The outstanding initial success was due, not only to the perfect co-operation between the Allied forces, but also to the great secrecy which had been maintained. Winston Churchill, in a speech to the House of Commons on November 11 revealed that orders for the expedition to French North Africa had been issued at the end of July, 1942. A vast convoy of ships had to be assembled to carry tens of thousands of troops and their fighting equipment to the landing grounds. This armada included more than 500 transports with about 350 protecting naval vessels. Powerful air cover was provided for the convoy all the time it was at sea and, despite the very great hazards of the route across the Atlantic and through the Western Mediterranean, all the ships arrived safely. The troops disembarked under cover of darkness and were convoyed from the transports to the beaches in auxiliary landing craft. The picture shows part of the huge convoy heading for Africa.

American eagles at rest in their nest enroute to Africa

PROTECTION FOR ALLIED CONVOY. Dauntless dive bombers of the U.S. Navy are lined up ready for action on the deck of an escort aircraft carrier in this great African convoy scene. Here, for miles, the

horizon is dotted with ships in this great movement of men and equipment, traveling under the protection of the planes, battleships and warships of the combined American and British fleets.

Casablanca feels the might of the A.E.F.

ASSAULT ON CASABLANCA. On November 10 French warships which offered resistance to the landing of the allies in Casablanca Harbor were fired on by allied warships and dive-bombed by allied planes,
Rear Admiral Hewitt, commander of the U.S. Naval forces throwing the whole of his fleet into the battle,
at the same time it was announced that the British land and air forces were operating with the Americans
in this campaign. An entire flotilla of French destroyers and lighter craft was wiped out, a French cruiser
was hit and badly damaged and the new 35,000-ton battleship, Jean Bart, was left in flames. Meanwhile
the allies continued their advance inland. On November 11 a conference was held at Algiers between
Lieut. General Mark Clark and Admiral Jean Darlan, after which the latter issued a proclamation ordering
all French land, sea and air forces to cease fighting against the Allies. It was also announced that members of the German Armistice Commission had been captured on November 9 by two British soldiers
while attempting to flee from Algiers. The pictures show: above, transports moving inshore while U.S.
soldiers await the order to transfer to the landing craft; top, right, a landing barge discharging troops; bottom, right, landing stores and equipment on a small beach to the west of Oran.

The British First army moves rapidly on Tunis

FIRST BATTLES IN TUNISIA. Afer the Allied landings in North Africa early in November the Germans seized control of Bizerta and Tunis and formed a strong defensive ring around them. On November 15 British and American advanced troops crossed the frontier into Tunisia. British paratroops were dropped at many key points, seizing airfields and taking prisoners. After preliminary tank and infantry clashes and the routing of an enemy mechanized column on November 20 heavy fighting developed as the Allies ad-

vanced towards the German fortified line west, south and east of Bizerta. On November 27, after overcoming stiff enemy resistance, the British First Army occupied Medjez-el-Bab, thirty-two miles west of Tunis. On the following day General Anderson pressed forward, with strong air support, for another seventeen miles and entered the town of Tebourba. By the capture of Djedeida on November 29, the First Army cut the rail line between Bizerta and Tunis. Photograph shows supplies being unloaded at Oran.

American tanks and tank destroyers in action in Tunisia

ADVANCE IN THE DESERT. An American tank of an armored division moves across the desert as the Allied advance into Tunisia gets under way. Immediately following the landings in North Africa, Axis forces were rushed into Tunisia by sea and air. As early as November 16, allied advance units encountered enemy patrols 60 miles west of Tunis. The leading units of the British First Army with American reinforcements of men and machinery, reached Medjez-el-Bab, 30 miles south of Tunis on November 25.

READY FOR THE FOE'S TANKS. An American tank destroyer company moving up to the front in the Tunisia sector over roads which are nothing but dust. On November 15, orders were issued for the movement of French troops then at Algiers and Constantine to protect the southern flank of the American and British units which were now advancing into Tunisia along the coastal corridors crossing the frontier. The French units were reinforced with American troops, including tank destroyers, as seen above.

How the enemy tried to block our tanks in North Africa

ATTEMPT TO SLOW-UP THE AMERICANS. A view of one of the streets in the shell-battered town of Sousse in which the enemy had placed tank obstructions in an effort to slow up the advance of the Allies. In the campaign for Tunisia there were considerable tank losses on both sides. The enemy was able to

maintain himself in his forward position by the use of extensive air power and delaying tactics and it was not until the spring of 1943 that the conquest of Tunisia was to be completed. This picture shows vividly the scenes of desolation which greeted the Allies in the captured town after the Nazi retreat.

Italian prisoners on the march

THE WAR ENDS FOR THEM. Headquarters Company of the First Division, United States Army, escorting Italian prisoners of war, seized during the Tunisia advance, to a stockade outside the town of El Guetter, in North Africa; in the picture at right, Lieut. General Mark W. Clark, (then a major general) who was in North Africa and Italy, is shown watching some of his troops marching up to the front. On November 27,

General Clark received the D. S. M. for his feat of slipping into French North Africa from a British submarine and conducting the preliminary negotiations which opened Algiers to American occupational forces. This was the second instance of official recognition bestowed upon the forty-six year old officer since the North African campaign started. The first was his advancement from Major General.

Red army stands firm in the Caucasus

FIGHTING IN THE CAUCASUS

Ever since August, 1942, the Germans had fought desperately to reach the oilfields of the Caucasus. After crossing the Kerch Straits from the Crimea they reached the Black Sea port of Anapa, twenty miles northwest of Novorossisk, on September 1. Another enemy force had already penetrated the mountains protecting Novorssisk from the north. On September 11, following a week of violent battles, the great naval base was evacuated by the Russians. Soviet Marines, co-operating with the Red Army and supported by the Black Sea Fleet, held the enemy's drive along the coastal road towards Tuapse. The Germans were unable to put the Russian Fleet out of action, despite its loss of important bases. Consequently, they were prevented from landing large invasion forces on this front. Meanwhile, the German armies advancing south to Tuapse through the mountains from Maikop made little progress. The most serious enemy advance was along the northern mountain slopes of the Caucasus towards the Grozny oilfield. This came within the Germans' grasp until, on September 8-12, they were halted on the Terek River by the Red Army. The Germans then brought up large Alpine troop reinforcements to attempt an out-flanking movement through Nalchik towards Ordzhonikidze at the end of the Georgian military highway Little progress was made, and everywhere enemy attacks were repulsed with heavy losses. By October 30, the Red Army had to withdraw near Nalchik owing to the pressure of numerically superior enemy forces and the town was evacuated on November 2. But the Russian positions on the Terek River held firm. It appeared that the Germans were trying to break through at Ordzhonikidze and gain control of the outlets to the Georgian and Ossetian military highways. By November 5 the advance beyond Nalchik was checked and the approaches to Ordzhonidikze held. The pictures show a Red Army patrol in the mountains.

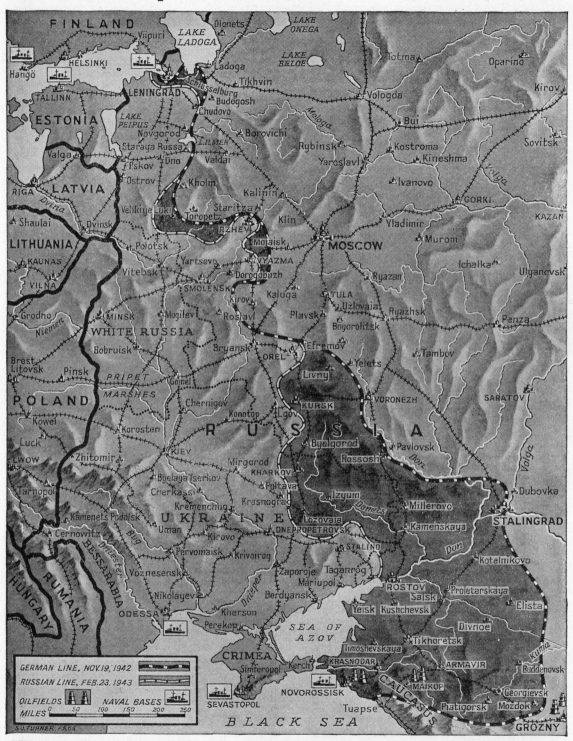

GERMANS RETREAT IN CAUCASUS. After weeks of fighting, the Red Army regained the initiative in the Caucasus on November 19. Their decisive victory near Mozdok lessened the serious threat to the Grozny oilfield. Here the Germans suffered a crushing defeat, losing 20,000 men killed and wounded. Booty captured by the Soviets included 140 tanks, 70 guns, 84 machine guns, and 2,350 trucks. The map shows the extent of the German push and the line to which they were forced to retreat three months later.

Germans retreat under Red army pressure  November 20, 1942

RUSSIAN REINFORCEMENTS MOVE FORWARD. On November 20 the Russians, continuing their offensive in the Caucasus, repulsed four enemy counter-attacks and wiped out a whole battalion of crack Rumanian infantry in a sector to the south-west of Mozdok. In the neighborhood of Ordzhonikidze the enemy were now in full retreat, abandoning one position after another with hardly a fight, while trying to retire into the cover of the mountain forests. The battered German divisions left behind thousands of dead and quantities of equipment and stores. Meanwhile, fresh Russian forces, trained for winter warfare, were sent from the east to strengthen the Red Army's powerful offensive on this front. The pictures show: above, a column of Russian infantry passing through a valley in the Caucasus Mountains, and, below, German soldiers reaching an important rail siding, only to discover that the oil tanks had been set ablaze.

French fleet scuttled in the harbor at Toulon

THE GLORY THAT WAS FRANCE. On November 27 German troops entered Toulon to seize the major part of the French fleet which lay in harbor there. But before they could reach the harbor the French naval commander, Admiral de Laborde, gave orders for all the ships to scuttle themselves. The captains stayed on the bridge until their ships went down, and many lost their lives. The scuttling of the French Mediterranean Fleet, in which 230,000 tons of naval shipping went to the bottom, was the greatest operation of its

kind since the German Fleet committed suicide at Scapa Flow in June, 1919. Among the warships destroyed were the 26,000-ton battleships Dunkerque and Strasbourg, the old 22,000-ton battleship Provence, the 10,000-ton cruisers Algerie, Colbert, Foch and Dupleix, and the 7,600-ton cruisers Jean de Vienne, La Galissonnaire, and La Marseillaise. Twenty-eight destroyers and twenty submarines were also sunk. The drawing by Charles Cundell, gives a striking impression of the scene at Toulon as the ships went down.

British and Americans forced back in Tunisia

GERMANS COUNTER-ATTACK IN TUNISIA. By December 1 the most bitter fighting in Tunisia was centered around Mateur and Djedeida where the Germans launched a heavy counter-attack with intensive air support. At first the enemy failed to break up the first Army's thrust between Bizerta and Tunis, but further counter-attacks caused the Allies to fall back. By ceaseless dive bombing and repeated tank attacks the enemy made all-out efforts to dislodge the British advance units before General Anderson was able to bring his main forces up to the battlefront. The Allies were at a disadvantage owing to local German air superiority, because their own air strength had not yet been fully brought into action. On December 4

enemy forces recaptured Djedeida and held it against attacks by British infantry and American tanks. Tebourba was evacuated by the British next day, when they retreated to entrenched positions overlooking the town in order to foil an enemy encircling movement. During these battles the Germans suffered heavy losses. Between December 1-3 no fewer than thirty-six of their tanks were destroyed and on December 6 twenty-one more were knocked out. Meanwhile Allied air strength continued to grow, although it was known that the Luftwaffe was also receiving reinforcements across the Mediterranean. The pictures show: left, a group of German parachutists taking cover and, right, how the enemy used Arabs for forced labor.

Rapid Russian advance across the River Don

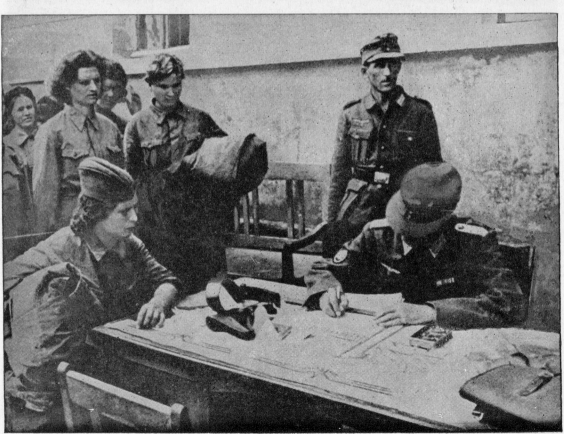

RUSSIAN ADVANCE CONTINUES

On December 5 the Red Army gained an important success when they recrossed the Don at several points in the Lower Don bend. Other Russian forces swooped down from the north and drove the Germans out of the towns of Sebretev and Parshin. So swift was the Red Army's advance on this front that by December 26 they had retaken Tatsyaskaya, an important road and rail junction 175 miles west of Stalingrad. Both Millerovo and the Voronezh-Rostov railways were now threatened. From December 16-26 the number of enemy prisoners rose by 6,300 to a total of 56,000 and war material captured included about 350 aircraft, 172 tanks and nearly 2,000 guns. The pictures show: top, left, German prisoners being marched away; bottom, left, Russian women soldiers being questioned after capture; bottom, right, Red Army men crossing the Don on collapsible floats.

The President Coolidge goes down in Pacific December 12, 1942

AMERICAN TROOPSHIP LOST. On December 12, while carrying troops to a destination in the Pacific, the President Coolidge hit an enemy mine off a small island in the Solomons group. Captain Henry Nelson, who was in command of the ship, rammed the stricken ship on to a coral reef. She slid off the reef, turned turtle and sank, but as a result of Captain Nelson's prompt action only two lives were lost, although there were 4,000 troops on board. The picture shows troops scrambling down cargo nets from the transport.

The assassination of Admiral Darlan

CHRISTMAS EVE TRAGEDY. On December 24, 1942, Admiral Jean Francois Darlan, 61 years old, self-appointed High Commissioner in French North and West Africa, who had been backed by the United States government as a "temporary expedient," was shot to death in Algiers by Bonnier de la Chapelle, 20 years old, member of a French patriotic youth organization, which aided Allied landings in North Africa. The young assassin was tried by court martial and was executed two days later. The assassination of Admiral Darlan precipitated a political crisis which was met by the action of the French North African Government in designating Gen. Henri Honore Giraud, military leader of the French troops as Darlan's successor. Admiral Darlan is shown, above, with General Eisenhower, Allied commander in chief.

Allied air supremacy makes itself felt in the desert

BRITISH AIR POWER IN THE DESERT. Following the routing of Rommel's armies at El Agheila on December 13, the R.A.F. kept up almost incessant day and night attacks on the fast retreating columns along the coastal road in Tripolitania. Whole lines of enemy transport and supply vehicles were wrecked, ammunition dumps were blown up, and airfields strafed from low levels. On December 15 day-long raids were carried out by British and American bombers on closely packed enemy columns about seventy miles west of El Agheila. At a place near "Marble Arch" blazing enemy vehicles caused a huge traffic block which delayed the retreating columns for many hours. Opposition from the Luftwaffe was negligible, but two enemy fighters were shot down. These far-reaching air attacks were made possible by the fine work of R.A.F. Ground Forces in clearing advanced airfields so recently in enemy hands. At one airfield 2,000 mines were removed from a landing field within forty-eight hours to make it serviceable for Allied bombers. The pictures show: above, twisted remains of aircraft on an enemy landing field in Libya, and, right, bullet-ridden Italian fighters and wrecked hangars at Castel Benito.

HEADACHES FOR ROMMEL. Huge American B-25 bombers fly low over their camp after taking off on a mission somewhere in North Africa. Bombers like these "softened up" Rommel's Mareth Line and played a large part in bringing about the Axis defeat in Tunisia. Despite all allied efforts, the short and easily maintained air and sea lines of communication between Sicily and Tunisia permitted the rapid build-up of Axis forces, however, his greatest advantage lay in the possession of all-weather airfields, as the development of the rainy season rendered fighter-plane support of Allied troops impossible.

SHATTERED BATTERIES. Blasted by demolition charges, the muzzles of these French 130 mm. guns present a picture of desolation on Pointe de la Tour, outside Safi, French Morocco. The guns were wrecked by their crews after their positions had been shelled by U.S. warships. Upon the cessation of hostilities in French territory, General Eisenhower's forces were faced with numerous and pressing problems. Harbors had to be cleared of sunken ships, wharfs and docks repaired, neglected and slender lines of rail communications had to be developed and civilians provided for and started on the way to reconstruction.

General MacArthur's men capture Buna village

JAPANESE DEFEATED IN PAPUA. After a month of the most desperate fighting in the South-West Pacific, American troops captured Buna village on December 14. During the night of the 13th a Japanese convoy attempted to land a relieving force from barges. But practically all the enemy were drowned or killed on the beaches by the heavy strafing inflicted by waves of Allied bombers. Fighting continued, however, in the small but strongly held Japanese salient round the Buna Mission, from which the enemy were not finally cleared until January 2. The photographs show: top, left, American reinforcements landing on Papua; bottom, left, Australian infantry in action; above, the shore at Buna Mission strewn with dead Japanese.

845

ADVANCE INTO TRIPOLITANIA

On December 16 the Eighth Army cut the retreating Afrika Korps in two by a brilliant outflanking movement at a place called Wadi Matratin, about sixty miles beyond El Agheila. This operation, which completely surprised the enemy, was actually planned by General Montgomery before the Battle of El Agheila, after British Intelligence officers had discovered a forgotten desert track running to the south and striking north to the coast road again along the Wadi Matratin. It was carried out by New Zealand troops under the command of General Freyberg, V.C. For three days the infantry advanced more than 100 miles over the desolate sand dunes and rocky wadis, supported by a strong force of artillery, tanks and armored cars. The trapped Axis rearguard, which was entirely composed of German troops, fought desperately in its attempt to break through the British armored ring. But although a few enemy troops and tanks managed to escape and join their main forces farther west, heavy punishment was inflicted by the New Zealanders. The enemy lost at least twenty tanks, thirty guns and several hundred motor vehicles. Five hundred Germans were taken prisoner. One of the most important results emerging from this action, according to a Cairo dispatch, was the capture or destruction of a very considerable amount of Rommel's motor transport and also appreciable numbers of his rearguard. On December 18 the Eighth Army after mopping-up operations, continued its advance from Wadi Matratin and came to within thirty miles of Sirte, almost half-way between Benghazi and Tripoli. The remarkable action picture on the left shows a small forward party of Australian infantry with bayonets and fire-arms advancing in the desert through a protective smoke screen after being detailed to capture a German strong point on the way towards Tripoli.

The Red army brings a White Christmas to the Caucasus

WINTER ADVANCE IN THE CAUCASUS. On December 25 the Red Army launched a new thrust against the enemy south-east of Nalchik and recaptured Alagir and Krasnogorsk, thereby regaining the use of the Ossetian military highway. Next day Russian ski troops advanced thirty miles across the snow and wiped out an enemy salient which still menaced the Grozny oilfields. On January 3, Mozdok, the important com-

munication center of the Caucasus, was retaken in a surprise attack by Cossack Guards. With Mozdok in Russian hands again the Grozny oilfields were denied to the invader. The picture shows a company of Russian ski troops on patrol. These soldiers played an important part in the Red Army's winter offensive. Time and again they tricked the Nazis because they were equipped with white uniforms and hoods.

EIGHTH ARMY ADVANCES TOWARDS TRIPOLI

Continuing to advance through Tripolitania, the Eighth Army chased the dwindling Afrika Korps along the coast road. The retreating enemy columns suffered continuous bombing from the air by the powerful Western Desert air force. On December 25, British troops occupied Sirte without opposition, but to the west of this town air operations were curtailed for a time owing to the bad weather conditions and violent sandstorms. Beyond the Wadi Bei-el-Kebir the Eighth Army's sappers were busily engaged for several days clearing away mines and booby traps which the Germans had strewn over the roads in great numbers in order to delay the advance. On January 5 our forces entered Buerat-el Hsun, about sixty miles west of Sirte where the coast road turns north along the salt marshes towards Misurata and Tripoli. After crossing the Wadi Zemzem on January 14, Eighth Army troops encountered enemy rearguards at a point seventy miles from Misurata, but Rommel soon abandoned all his defensive positions in this area. Four days later Misurata was occupied without any opposition, by January 20 the Eighth Army had progressed along the coast beyond Misurata to the important defensive positions of Homs and Tahuna, and on the following day advanced British columns had entered the suburbs of Tripoli, whose capture was announced less than forty-eight hours afterwards. Meanwhile heavy day and night blows were delivered against Tripoli harbor and the great Axis airfield at Castel Benito on the outskirts of the city. The picture, left, shows British infantry advancing behind tanks in Tripolitania.

Tanks which helped change the tide of battle for the Allies

ARMORED DIVISION IN TRAINING. As the year 1943 opened, tanks and armored units were to play a more important part in the Allied plans. The pictures on these two pages show the crew of a British

armored division being trained under conditions made highly realistic by smoke bombs, high explosives and modern tactics in an effort to beat the Nazis at their own game.

MacArthur's troops gain control of Buna Mission

JAPANESE RESISTANCE ENDS AT BUNA

On January 2, Allied troops occupied the Government Station at Buna in New Guinea after shattering the Japanese defenses there. By this victory the battle for Buna was virtually brought to an end after six weeks of the most bitter fighting amid swamps and jungles in one of the worst climates in the world. The last remaining point of enemy resistance in the Buna area was a small pocket to the west of the Giropa creek. There the Japanese continued to fight on desperately for several days until they were finally cut off by an American force which joined the Australians after the latter had taken the Government Station. Such was the ferocity of the fighting at Buna itself that on the last day 650 Japanese soldiers were killed. Enemy troops which tried to escape from the coast by swimming were attacked from the air by Kittyhawk fighters. By January 3, all organized resistance in the Buna area had ended, but Allied troops continued to mop up groups of isolated snipers. A few miles west of Buna, small Japanese forces still showed resistance at Sanananda Point, but owing to heavy rains and swollen swamps ground operations here were seriously hindered for many days. On January 17, however, Allied troops cut the main road in two places behind the enemy's rear, less than 2,000 yards from the coast and thereby split the remaining Japanese forces into three isolated groups. By the next day two headlands on either side of Sanananda Point had been captured and the enemy were now hemmed into a 500-yard strip of coast and a few isolated and surrounded pockets inland. Despite tropical rains and floods Allied progress continued and on January 22, the last remaining Japanese positions at Sanananda fell and the reconquest of the Papuan part of New Guinea was completed. About 750 Japanese were killed in the final attack and a great quantity of military equipment and stores was captured. The picture shows Japanese killed and drowned on the beach at Buna Mission with a smashed landing boat in the background.

Reunion at Casablanca—Roosevelt and Churchill meet again

ALLIED CONFERENCE AT CASABLANCA. On January 14, the President of the United States and the Prime Minister of Great Britain met at Casablanca in French Morocco, for important discussions on the future Allied operations in the war. They were accompanied by the combined Chiefs of Staff of the two countries and their expert advisers. This was the fourth wartime meeting of the two great Allied leaders. Although Marshal Stalin was invited to join in the talks he was unable to leave Russia owing to the offensive operations of the Red Army which he was directing. Nevertheless, he was fully informed of the decisions made, one of the objectives of which was to relieve pressure on the Russian forces. The far-reaching importance of this meeting in North Africa may be judged by the fact that it was the greatest gathering of Allied war chiefs called since the oubreak of the Second World War. Mr. Churchill left Britain on January 12 in the same Liberator which took him on his 14,000-mile trip to the Middle East and Moscow in August, 1942. President Roosevelt arrived in North Africa on January 14 after making the 5,000-mile flight across the Atlantic by Clipper. During the conference, which lasted ten days, the whole field of the Second World War was surveyed in detail, and all Allied resources were marshalled for the more intense prosecution of the war by land, sea and air. President Roosevelt, Mr. Churchill and their respective staffs arrived at complete agreement regarding plans for offensive operations which were to be undertaken by the Allies against the Axis in the 1943 campaign. The conference also provided an opportunity for a meeting between the Fighting French leaders, Generals de Gaulle and Giraud. These Casablanca pictures show: top, left, General Nogues (France) and General Patton (U.S.A.); bottom, left, President with Mr. Churchill; above, Generals de Gaulle and Giraud.

The glory that was Rome fades in the African desert

BRITISH ENTER TRIPOLI. At 5 a.m. on January 23 the victorious Eighth Army entered Tripoli and the Union Jack was hoisted from a fort overlooking the harbor. Thus the last remaining capital of Mussolini's former empire passed into British hands, three months to the day since the offensive began at El Alamein. The final advance on the city came from three directions. Two columns of armored units and New Zealand infantry pushed through the desert to the south, while the British infantry advanced from the east along the coast road. Most of the inhabitants of the city lined the streets as columns of British tanks, armored vehicles and infantry filed into the main square from the suburbs. At midday General Montgomery received the official surrender of Tripoli from the Vice-Governor of Libya at a point just outside the city walls. Since the attack at El Alamein the Eighth Army had advanced 1,400 miles in ninety days to reach Tripoli, an average of nearly sixteen miles a day in most difficult country and often in bad weather. The pictures show: top, left, British tanks entering Tripoli; bottom, left, a party of Gordon Highlanders, with the harbor behind them; above, hoisting the British flag over the harbor.

LONGEST DESERT MARCH. On January 30 a mechanized force of Fighting French under General Leclerc reached Tripoli after a hazardous journey of 1,700 miles across the Sahara from the Chad territory of Central Africa. From their headquarters at Fort Lamy, near Lake Chad, they advanced into southern Libya, attacking many Italian outposts with the support of the French air force. On January 6, El Gatrun was stormed by a camel corps detachment under Captain Saruzac. Much booty and 177 Italian prisoners were taken. On January 10, General Leclerc's G.H.Q. announced the capture of El Gatrun and Brach, another enemy outpost in the Fezzan oasis. The conquest of the Fezzan was completed on January 12 with the capture of Murzouk, the capital, and Sebha, the chief military base. On January 27, the Free French joined with another force under General Giraud at Ghadames to undertake further operations. The photograph shows General Leclerc with two of his men.

AXIS TROOPS CLEARED FROM LIBYA. Advancing still westwards from Tripoli the Eighth Army maintained contact with enemy rearguards and on January 31 occupied the port of Zuara, the last Italian town on the Tripolitanian coast. Meanwhile, advanced British patrols had already crossed the frontier into Tunisia to the south of the coastal road. On February 2, a fifteen-mile advance was made from Zuara to the village of Zelten, beyond which artillery duels were exchanged with the Axis forces withdrawing towards Pisada, only twelve miles from the Tunisian frontier. For the next two weeks progress was slower and operations on land were reduced to patrol activity until, on February 15, the Eighth Army occupied Ben Gardane and its big airfield and began the advance towards Medenine and the Mareth Line. The photographs show: above, British 6-pounder anti-tank gun in action; and below, British infantry moving to capture an enemy strong point under cover of a damaged German tank.

Convoy survivors rescued after battle with U-boats

GREAT ATLANTIC CONVOY BATTLE. On March 18, the British issued the account of one of the greatest winter battles of the Atlantic between a pack of U-boats and convoy escorts. The battle, which lasted for three days and nights in February, was fought out by British, U.S., and Fighting French escort ships, together with Liberator and Sunderland aircraft. The convoy did not escape without loss, but heavy damage was inflicted on the U-boats, three of which were sunk and many others probably

sunk. The picture on left shows some of the survivors from one of the torpedoed ships being assisted aboard a rescuing vessel. The picture above shows the rescue of three British seamen from a raft on which they had lived for eighty-three days before being sighted and picked up by a U.S. Navy patrol boat. Two other companions had died on the raft and were buried at sea. The three castaways who **survived had lived—or existed—for almost twelve weeks on fish, birds and rainwater.**

Rapid construction of America's "Burma Road"

NEW ROAD TO TOKIO. The U.S. State Department announced on March 18, 1942, a Canadian-U.S. agreement for the construction, under the auspices of the Joint Defense Board, of the Alaska Highway linking the Continental United States with Alaska via British Columbia and Yukon. Work on America's "Burma Road" was begun at once and despite climatic and physiographic difficulties, 10,000 soldiers and 6,000 civilian workers under the direction of the U.S. Public Roads Administration pushed the construction work ahead at the rate of eight miles a day, bridging some 200 streams and laying the twenty-four foot wide roadway over mountain ranges, rivers and bogs. Intended to be in use by the end of the year the highway was designed to be one of the most important lines of communication for reinforcing Allied forces in the Pacific, as well as to carry supplies to Russia and China with practically no risk. The picture above, gives some impression of the obstacles which had to be blasted from the path of the highway. Those on the right show: above, the highway in use at a point where transport drivers may obtain rest and refreshment; and below, another section driven through virgin forest.

The final offensive on Guadalcanal gets under way

ALLIES ON THE OFFENSIVE IN PACIFIC. The importance which the Japanese had attached to the Solomons, and especially to the island of Guadalcanal, where their construction of bases for the intended attack upon Australia was interrupted by the U.S. landing in August 1942, was revealed by the repeated attempts they made between then and February 1943 to regain control of the island. The strongest of these attempts, launched regardless of losses, involved the occupying U.S. forces and their protecting air and naval units in some of the toughest fighting of the whole Pacific campaign before it was finally announced on February 9 from Tokio that Japanese troops had been evacuated from Guadalcanal. The pictures show: top, left, U.S. marines engaged in the task of mopping-up the island during the final offensive on Guadalcanal which was launched on January 15; below, a command car of the American Army being ferried across a jungle river. Above, American troops in action on a gun site.

Americans drive the Japanese from Guadalcanal Island

U.S. VICTORY ON GUADALCANAL. On February 10 it was announced from Washington that the whole of Guadalcanal island was under American control. For six months it had been the scene of heavy fighting between U.S. forces and the Japanese. The loss of this vital Pacific base was a severe defeat for the enemy. The Henderson airfield, which the Japanese had almost completed when U.S. marines landed on Guadalcanal in August, 1942, was intended as an air base for the invasion of Australia The campaign cost the enemy 75,000 men, 800 aircraft and 166 warships and transports. During the final offensive, which began on January 15, U.S. troops killed more than 6,000 of the enemy, captured 130 prisoners and vast quantities of material. The pictures show: above, an American landing barge at Guadalcanal and, right, troops bathing on the island.

Bestial Nazi policy of extermination in Poland

NAZI TERROR IN POLAND

On July 9 the Polish Government in London issued a statement describing the pitiable fate of Poles and Jews under the terror regime of the Nazi occupying forces. Within the past year, declared the Polish Deputy Premier, the number of Poles and Jews murdered had increased to 400,-000, and in the months following Himmler's visit to Warsaw in March, the Gestapo had intensified their terror severely. The setting up of the ghetto in Warsaw in 1940 was later followed by the establishment of similar colonies in practically every Polish town and village. The Jewish death-rate in Warsaw alone was estimated at 6,000 weekly, and exhaustion, starvation and disease were systematically exterminating the Jewish population. The totally inadequate supplies of food for the inhabitants of these ghettos led to smuggling on a large scale, and the Germans themselves participated in this illicit trading. The consequences of this privation were particularly tragic during winter months, when scores of corpses were collected from the streets of the ghetto every day. The pictures below and above, right, among the first to reach this country, reveal something of the desolation and misery in which inhabitants of the Warsaw ghetto eked out their precarious existence; above, left, a grim cameo of the New Order in Poland shows Polish peasants lined up awaiting the execution squad. The man on the left of the picture is one of the many Polish priests against whom the Nazi terrorists vented their brutal wrath.

Great German winter retreat in Russia

KURSK AND KHARKOV RECAPTURED. Immediately following the expulsion of the enemy from Voronezh the Red Army advanced rapidly for nearly forty miles on a broad front and liberated some 200 inhabited places in this area. These included the vital railway junction of Kastornaya and the town of Novy Oskol, both of which were heavily defended and fell only after bitter hand-to-hand fighting in the streets. On February 4 further gains in this sector brought the Russians to within thirty miles of Kursk which was encircled by them on three sides. This great German bastion was captured on February 8 after tremendous tank and infantry battles, and its loss endangered the whole German position in south Russia. Meanwhile, on the Donetz front farther south, fighting raged on the outskirts of Kharkov, the capital of the Ukraine. Despite the most stubborn German resistance by troops which included the "Adolf Hitler" tank division, the Russians, supported by great formations of dive bombers, smashed their way into the center of the city on February 16. Picked SS. troops, rushed from France to Kharkov only two weeks previously, were crushingly defeated and thousands were slain. The pictures show: above, aftermath of battle in a Russian village; right, German troops firing homes of Russian peasants.

Red army continues to advance in the Ukraine

GERMANS DRIVEN FROM ROSTOV AND VOROSHILOVGRAD. On February 14 after several days of violent house and street fighting, the Red Army recaptured the vitally important city of Rostov-on-Don for the second time. The renowed Cossack Guards Division, under the command of Col.-Gen. Malinovski, led the final and decisive assault against the city from the south-west bank of the Don. Rostov had been in the enemy's hands for practically six months. On the same day General Vatutin's forces won another great victory with the reoccupation of the industrial city of Voroshilovgrad after a furious battle which raged without interruption for forty-eight hours. During this battle the Red Army had to force a way through some 3,000 blockhouses and an elaborate network of anti-tank traps which the Germans had built during their occupation. The arrival of the Red Army brought shouts of joy from thousands of Russian peasants. The pictures show: left, peasants returning to Rostov; above, a Russian family mourning a relative killed by the Germans; below, some of the refugees awaiting return to their homes.

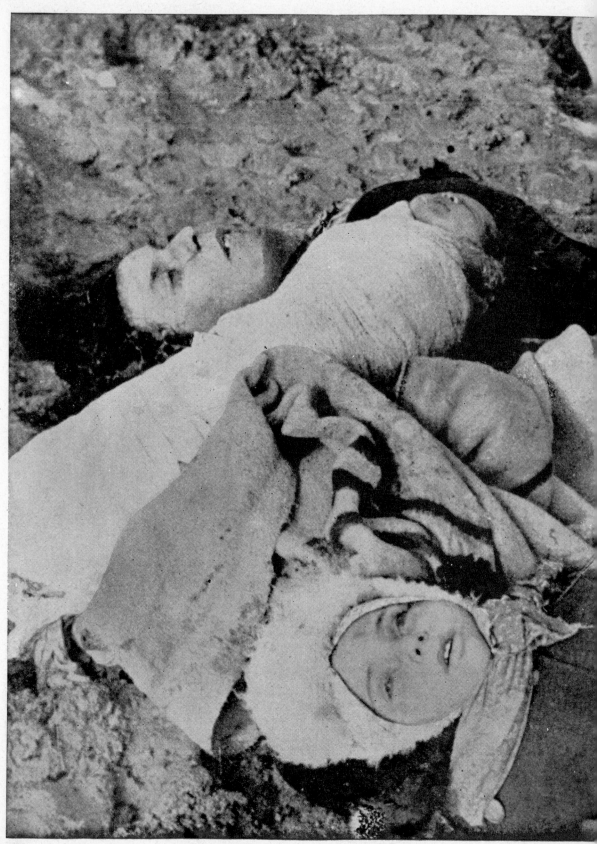

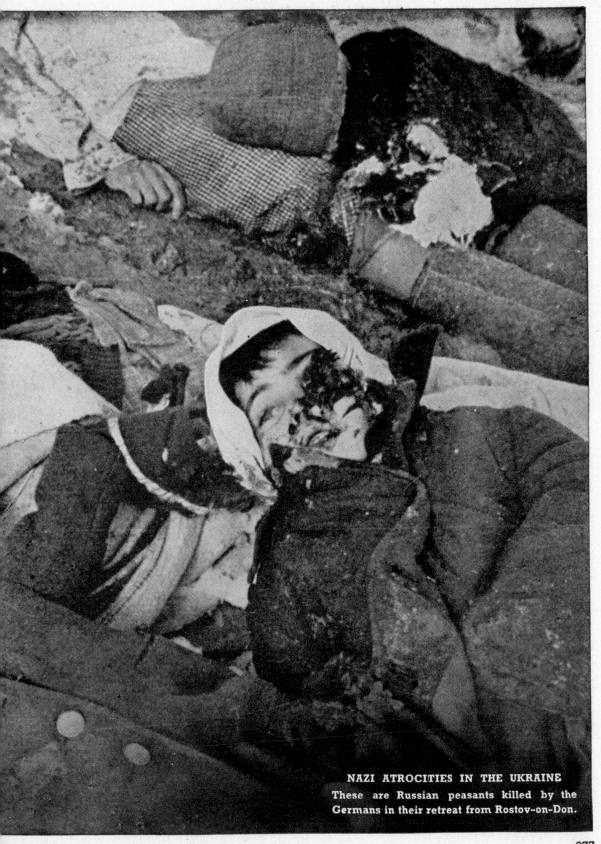

NAZI ATROCITIES IN THE UKRAINE
These are Russian peasants killed by the
Germans in their retreat from Rostov-on-Don.

Allied navies improve anti-submarine measures

GROWING SUCCESS AGAINST U-BOATS. During the most critical period of the war at sea the enemy employed packs of U-boats to lurk in the path of Allied convoys. These new methods of the Germans, however, were successfully countered and the 600-mile danger gap in the Atlantic became less hazardous. The great strain under which U-boat crews worked is evident from the picture, right, which shows a crew waiting in suspense, listening to depth charges. The picture above shows an Allied destroyer about to drop its depth charges in an endeavor to bag one of the Atlantic prowlers.

American forces temporarily set back in Tunisia

U.S. TROOPS FALL BACK IN TUNISIA. On February 14, while the Eighth Army was pushing forward to Medenine after capturing Ben Gardane, the Germans launched a strong attack against the relatively lightly held American lines in the central part of Tunisia. The attack was delivered by a German armored division in two columns. Supported by masses of fighter aircraft and dive bombers, the Germans quickly overran the advanced American positions and completely isolated some artillery and infantry units. Counter-attacks somewhat delayed the enemy's advance, but Axis reinforcements were brought up in very strong force with the result that the U.S. troops were compelled to evacuate the Gafsa Oasis and also three of their forward airfields—one at Sbeitla and two at Telepte. After four days of fierce fighting the Americans were pushed back about thirty-five miles from the advanced positions they had previously held. The pictures show: top, left, the American-built Priest gun-howitzer in action; bottom, left, troops moving up through the enemy barrage; above, a camouflaged British gun.

German assault on Thala stemmed by Allied Forces

DESPERATE FIGHTING IN TUNISIA. On February 21, having advanced thirty miles since they moved out from the Faïd Pass, the Germans pierced the new shorter line held by the U.S. forces with a heavy Panzer attack. Thereafter they increased their pressure, and their mechanized and infantry columns made three strong assaults against Sbiba, Thala and towards Tebessa. The strongest attack, made with over seventy tanks and infantry, brought them to within a few miles of the key mountain town of Thala. British tanks and infantry were sent as reinforcements. After desperate fighting the Allies succeeded in holding the Axis thrust, inflicting severe casualties and taking prisoners. On the first day a score of enemy tanks were knocked out. The next day the British brought into action for the first time a number of 40-ton Churchill tanks, and these inflicted considerable losses on the enemy. In one of these tank battles nine Churchills took on fourteen German tanks and destroyed four of them. Only one of the British tanks was lost. On February 23 the Germans were forced to withdraw. Allied success in recapturing the ground they had lately lost was largely due to heavy attacks by their combined air forces from bases in the rear. The pictures show: above, British infantry attacking; right, shell bursting on German tank.

German attacks repulsed in Northern Tunisia

BRITISH REGAIN GROUND IN THE NORTH. On February 26, while the enemy was hastily withdrawing from the Kasserine Pass, a heavy attack was launched against the British First Army in the north. No fewer than six separate attacks were made with 5,000 troops, including parachutists, with strong tank support. All of them, however, were repulsed and the enemy suffered a major defeat. More than 400 German prisoners were taken and many of their tanks and heavy guns knocked out. Nevertheless,

the enemy continued to attack on an eighty-mile front from Cape Serrat to Jebel Mansour, south-east of Bou Arada. Again he was thrown back at every point with heavy losses in men and material. In particular, the Churchill tanks inflicted serious punishment on the enemy's armored columns. By March 2 the British forces had regained all the important points and the enemy, having suffered such grave casualties, reduced the momentum of his attacks. The picture shows British troops crossing a ford.

Russians drive the Nazis out of Rzhev and Vyazma

RUSSIA'S MIGHTY STRUGGLE. On a continuous front of over 1,000 miles Russia's fight against the invader never slackened in its fierce intensity. The German hope that the spring thaw would slow down the Red Army's advance proved unfounded. On March 3 the Germans were driven out of Rzhev (140 miles north-west of Moscow) with losses of 2,000 killed, and of booty including 112 tanks, 78 guns, and over 1,000 railway coaches. Rzhev had been so well fortified that to capture it by flank or frontal assault had been thought impossible; but the German commander, knowing that the Russians were grouping for a gigantic offensive, decided to evacuate the town. To hinder pursuit the Germans dynamited the bridges over the Volga. Advancing in the Northern Ukraine, Soviet troops had successes, capturing Lgov, fifty miles west of Kursk, and Dmitriev, thirty miles north of Lgov. On March 12 the Russians stormed Vyazma, and continued their drive towards Smolensk, the biggest German base in Russia. In the battles for Vyazma German losses were 9,000 killed. Pictures: above, the path of the Nazi retreat; top, right, Germans retreat through the snows; bottom, right, Russian troops with machine guns on sleds.

CHINA ON THE OFFENSIVE

On March 15 the Chinese High Command announced a great victory on the Yangtse River front to the west of Hankow. A few days earlier more than 20,000 Japanese troops crossed the river in eight columns ready to launch an offensive towards Hankow. On March 13, however, a general Chinese counter-offensive was begun, and after less than two days fighting the enemy was flung back in disorder and full retreat. Several places of strategic importance were recaptured in the province of Hupeh. This splendid victory showed that even after six years of brutal warfare the spirit of China's fighting forces was still high despite their isolation from the Allies, their serious lack of equipment and widespread famine among the civilian population. Nevertheless, in the spring of 1943 Generalissimo Chiang Kai-shek had some 5,000,000 fighting men under his command and another 15,000,000 men standing in reserve, trained and awaiting equipment. Nearly another 20,000,000 had received preliminary militia training. The great bulk of these Chinese armies was recruited from the peasant classes. This, in fact, was a source of their strength. For, being bred in the countryside, every man was well acquainted with the terrain in which he had to fight and was tough enough to cover the distances involved in the campaigns against the enemy. Since the Japanese began what they called the China "incident" the Chinese had made rapid strides with the development of their own war industries. As the "incident" approached its seventh year there were nearly 2,000 arms factories in parts of the country remote from enemy attack with thousands of trained women to work in them. Picture shows supply barges on the Yangtse.

Allied armored forces rout German panzers

BATTLES OF THE TANKS

In the Tunisian fighting the armored divisions of both sides played a considerable part, and their support was indispensable to secure the full exploitation of any break through of opposing forces. On March 6, the enemy made a heavy assault on British positions in Southern Tunisia with infantry and tanks. It failed signally. The enemy forces were compelled to withdraw towards the hills to the north of Medenine, and in one day's fighting thirty-three Axis tanks were destroyed without a single British tank being lost. Two days later enemy tanks captured by the British totalled fifty. At the end of February the important Kasserine Pass, which had seen much bitter fighting when it had been taken from the Allies by a very heavy Panzer attack a week earlier, was successfully cleared of the enemy and was once again in Allied hands. American and British infantry, supported by tanks, forced this enemy withdrawal. Among the prisoners who surrendered were many Italians. As the Eighth Army advanced and the number of enemy prisoners increased, the ratio of captured Italians to Germans was, on many occasions, found to be six to one, showing that the Germans had no compunction in deserting the soldiers of Italy, then their ally. The pictures on these pages show some incidents during this stage of the fighting in Tunisia: top, British tank crews mounting before an advance against enemy positions; bottom, hundreds of war-weary Italian soldiers surrendering to the Eighth Army.

The Eighth army attacks the Mareth defenses

BATTLE OF THE MARETH LINE. On the night of March 20-21 the Eighth Army began a full-scale attack on the Mareth Line along a six-mile front between the sea and the Medenine-Gabes road. After thirty-six hours of fierce hand-to-hand fighting all preliminary objectives had been gained and British infantry, strongly supported by masses of tanks and aircraft, had driven a wide bridgehead into the north part of the line between Mareth and Zarat. As at El Alamein, General Montgomery delivered a frontal assault

against the enemy's most vital sector and strengthened this assault by heavy artillery attack and air bombardment. During the first phase of the operations 1,700 prisoners, nearly all of them German, were captured. For some days bitter and bloody fighting ensued and the enemy suffered heavy casualties. On March 28, the Eighth Army captured Mareth, Toujane and Matmata and the entire Mareth Line fell into Allied hands. The photograph shows a section of British artillery shelling the Mareth defenses.

EIGHTY-THREE DAYS ON A RAFT. Wary of a possible trap, a U.S. patrol boat approaches cautiously to find three ragged, starved men on an 8' x 10' raft floated on two empty oil drums. The only American, 21-year old Basil Dominic Izzi, South Barry, Mass., an armed guard crew member, feebly hails the on-coming craft, the first seen by the trio since the thirty-fifth day of their 83-day saga. Izzi's companions are both Hollanders. Two other Americans died on the raft and were buried at sea by their companions, the victims of a Nazi wolf pack that had been plying the South Atlantic during the spring of 1943.

CURTAINS FOR AN ENEMY TANK. This dramatic picture was taken just as an R.A.F. plane scored a direct bomb hit on this German tank, filling the air with flying steel, smoke and clouds of desert sand. The efforts of the R.A.F. during the drive through the desert were of tremendous value to the Allies as they made it practically impossible for the enemy to bring up supplies to their sorely harassed troops.

CROSSING THE WADI ZIGZAU. In order to reach their preliminary objectives in the Mareth Line on March 20-22, British infantry columns had to fight their way across the rocky precipices of the Wadi Zigzau in the face of bitter opposition from the enemy. This wadi was the toughest natural obstacle the Eighth Army had encountered since the earliest days of their advance from Egypt. Yet Royal Engineers managed to bridge it under fierce enemy fire. The picture shows a British casualty being treated.

Eighth army breaks through the Mareth line   March 28, 1943

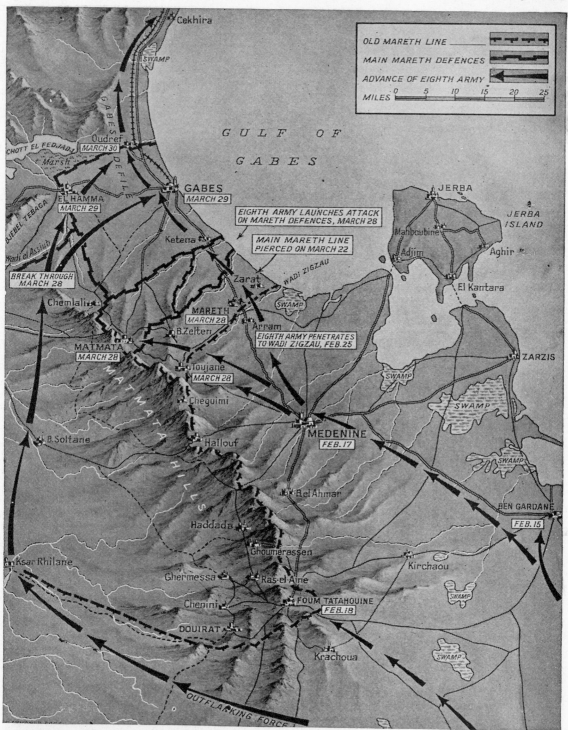

BIG OUTFLANKING MOVEMENT. After the capture of Medenine on February 17 the Eighth Army advanced to the Wadi Zigzau, a deep gorge forming part of the Mareth defense system. It proved to be such a tough obstacle that General Montgomery sent a wide outflanking force round the south of the Matmata Hills. On March 28 this outflanking force broke through strong enemy defense positions along the Wadi el Assiub. Meanwhile, Allied forces in the coastal sector occupied the whole Mareth Line.

BATTLE OF AKARIT

The Eighth Army in Tunisia lost no time after its victory at Mareth. Only eight days after it had successfully broken the Mareth Line it gained a new victory. In the pitch darkness of a moonless night, on April 6, General Montgomery's main forces attacked the strongly fortified position of Akarit, north of Gabes, and battered their way to success after heavy and bitter fighting. The advance of the British and Indian infantry was preceded and covered by a terrific artillery barrage—the heaviest yet known in Southern Tunisia—from 500 guns. Within a few hours General Montgomery's troops wore down the enemy's determined resistance, captured the two key hills, Djebel Houmana and Djebel Fatnassa, on each side of his positions, and forced a gap in the enemy's line enabling the armored forces to pass through. Fierce counter-attacks by the enemy were successfully repulsed, and by nightfall British tank squadrons had reached open country and were in pursuit of the retreating enemy. Six thousand prisoners were taken as a result of the first day's operations, and this fresh success by the Eighth Army enabled its troops to link forces with the Second U.S. Army Corps at Djebel Chemse, east of El Guettar. Most of the prisoners taken were Italians. Following up this success, the Eighth Army pushed forward along the coast, and on April 8 reached Cekhira, overlooking the Tunisian plain, an advance of fifteen miles from the Wadi Akarit line. It was now evident that the Afrika Korps was in full retreat. The fleeing enemy columns were harassed remorselessly by heavy and continuous air attack by bombers and fighter bombers of the Tactical Air Force. These wrecked or damaged great numbers of tanks and transport vehicles on the northern roads to Sfax, which British troops reached on April 10, having covered over fifty miles since the attack on Akarit began. The number of prisoners captured had now mounted to 10,000. This picture shows a dead Nazi beside his gun.

The ports of Sfax and Sousse fall to the Eighth army

EIGHTH ARMY STRIKES NORTH AGAIN. After it had captured the port of Sfax on April 10, the Eighth Army pushed on northwards over most difficult marshy country which the enemy had sown profusely with mines and booby traps. Nevertheless, in spite of these obstacles the advance was rapid over the eighty-mile stretch to Sousse, which was entered on April 12. Sousse, the third largest port in Tunisia, was occupied without opposition, although the enemy had destroyed all the port and dock installations and the town's electricity and water supplies before evacuating. While Rommel's armies had suffered further heavy casualties during and since the retreat from the Mareth Line, the greater part of that which remained of the Afrika Korps, nevertheless, escaped northwards into the high ground to the north of Enfidaville. Since March 20, when the attack on the Mareth Line opened, the Eighth Army alone had taken a further 20,000 prisoners in Tunisia. The pictures show: left, sappers of the Eighth Army repairing a bridge over the river at Gabes, which was blown up by the Germans as they retreated northwards; right, General Montgomery is seen entering the port of Sousse after its capture.

Action by the Americans on the road to Tunis

ON THE DOUBLE. Members of the Rifle Brigade of the 1st Armored Division storming enemy positions, the last opposition before reaching Tunis, near Kounine Hills, Tunis. On April 15, General Eisenhower announced that Axis losses in the Tunisian campaign included 66,000 killed, wounded or captured;

250 tanks, 3,000 vehicles and 425 guns destroyed or captured; 1,754 planes destroyed and 586 damaged —a total of 2,618 put out of action. The Allied advance was mile by mile, in terrific hand to hand fighting, as shown in the above picture, and losses on both sides were necessarily heavy.

CAPTURE OF FERRYVILLE

On 7 May, American forces entered Ferryville on the south shore of the Lake of Bizerta. Here is shown the great damage caused to the harbour by Allied air attack. On left of the jetty are the remains of an Italian 6,000-ton ammunition ship after a direct hit. After the explosion, parts of the ship were picked up miles away

Prisoner of war camp and some prize "catches"

THE PATHS OF GLORY END. Aerial view of a Prisoner of War Camp near Mateur, North Africa. Equipped to take care of 40,000 prisoners, more than 9,000 were taken by the Allies on the day this picture was taken. Truckloads of the prisoners are shown arriving at their destination. By the time of the fall of Tunis in May, 1943, more than 252,000 Axis troops had surrendered, 48,000 of them taken by the French.

FAREWELL TO ARMS. German generals arriving at the prisoner of war camp. Among the generals were: General Von Quast, Major General Von Vaerst, General Bieldwius, Major General Basseage, Major General Borowletz, Major General Krause and Major General Neuffer. In accordance with terms of the Geneva convention, which prescribes treatment of prisoners, these officers were granted full honors.

Tunis and Bizerte fall to the Americans and British

ALLIED ARMIES CAPTURE TUNIS AND BIZERTE. At dawn on May 6 the British First Army, supported by masses of bombers and fighter bombers, launched the final offensive for Tunis from the south of the river Mejerda, east of Medjez-el-Bab. A few hours later tanks, armored cars and infantry had broken through the strongly fortified German positions at Massicault, sixteen miles from the city of Tunis. The British armored columns then rolled on into the Tunisian plain, and on the afternoon of May 7 advanced elements of the First Army entered Tunis. They had covered about twenty-three miles in thirty-six hours despite stiff enemy resistance. Meanwhile, in the north the American and French troops, who began their offensive at precisely the same time as the British, were making equally rapid progress to Bizerte. An American force advancing northwards from Mateur cleared the enemy's stronghold on Jebel Achkel, on the south shore of Lake Achkel. After the capture of Ferryville, the Second U.S. Corps poured into Bizerte at 4 p.m. on May 7. The pictures show: top, left, American tanks driving past smashed German guns; bottom, left a British patrol marches into Tunis; above an American patrol enters Bizerte on the alert.

STREET FIGHTHING IN TUNIS. Although the main body of the enemy had fled from Tunis by the time that British troops began to enter the city soon after noon on May 7, many German snipers' nests had to be cleared up. German sappers were also blowing up munition dumps and installations. Consequently street fighting went on in the suburbs for many hours before all enemy resistance was liquidated. The pictures show: above, British Bren gunners in action in Tunis; below, German prisoners being marched away.

The enemy trapped at Cape Bon

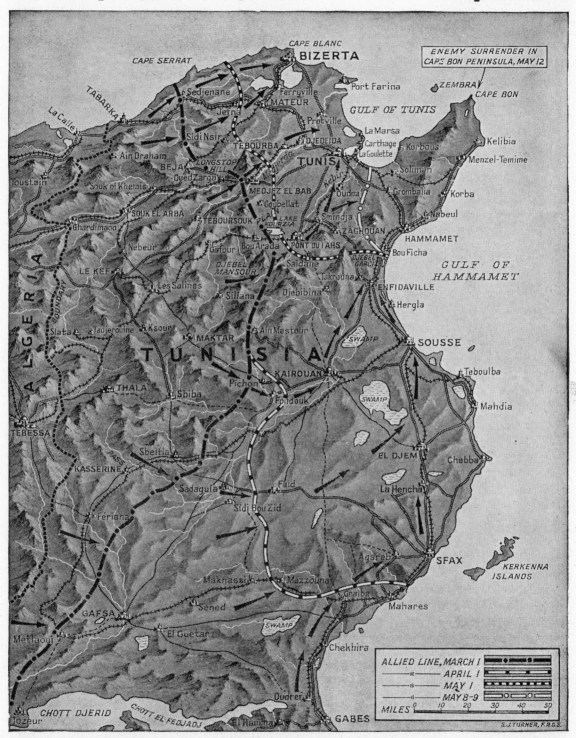

AXIS RETREAT IN TUNISIA. This map shows the stages of the Allied advance through Tunisia in the last two months of the campaign. Arrows indicate the main thrusts against the enemy: in the south by the Eighth Army, in the center through the Kasserine Pass and Pichon by the First Army and Americans, and in the north the final British and U.S. drive on Tunis and Bizerte. The Axis forces were pushed back with increasing speed in April, and were trapped on Cape Bon peninsula, where they surrendered on May 12.

Allies advance to the Cape Bon Peninsula and victory

ENEMY RETREAT TOWARDS CAPE BON. By the capture of Tunis and Bizerte the whole Axis defense system in the center and northern parts of Tunisia was broken and their remaining forces cut into two. On the following day, May 8, British armored units made progress in a north-easterly direction from Tunis, linking up with American armored units of the U.S. 2nd Corps advancing from Bizerte and Mateur. Farther south a force of Fighting French, operating with part of the British First Army, fought its way over many miles of difficult country and occupied the important town of Zaghouan. Meanwhile, in the most southerly sector, the Eighth Army, which had repulsed a small enemy attack north-west of Enfidaville on the previous day, made good progress and captured a large number of prisoners. Except at the entrances to the Cape Bon peninsula only a few isolated pockets of enemy resistance were left in Tunisia. The pictures on these pages, which were taken on the day before the fall of Tunis, show: top, left, British infantry take an enemy mortar position; bottom, left, a German killed beside his gun; above, British advancing under fire.

Churchill in America for fifth meeting with Roosevelt

CHURCHILL VISITS ROOSEVELT

It was officially announced on May 11 that Prime Minister Churchill had arrived in Washington at the invitation of President Roosevelt. This was the fifth wartime meeting of the two leaders. It took place earlier than had been expected because the sweeping Allied successes in North Africa—enemy resistance in the Cape Bon peninsula had collapsed and the surrender of the Axis forces remaining in Tunisia was imminent—necessitated conference and discussion upon the great problem of where Allied forces would make their next large-scale attack. A full review of the mighty problems of armaments, supply, and transport for that attack was essential. Mr. Churchill's days in the American capital were taken up with meetings with political and service leaders and talks with President Roosevelt. Broadcasting to Britain from the White House, May 14, on the occasion of the third anniversary of the Home Guard, Mr. Churchill left no doubt as to the purpose of the momentous conferences which were being held. "We are gathered here now, with the highest professional authorities in all the fighting services of the two great English-speaking nations, to plan well ahead of the armies who are moving swiftly forward. We must prepare for the time which is approaching and will surely come, when the bulk of these armies will have advanced across the seas into deadly grapple on the Continent." On May 19, in a speech to a joint session of the United States Congress, the Prime Minister declared: "Britain will wage war by America's side against Japan while there is breath in our bodies and while blood flows in our veins." He also gave Axis losses in Africa as 950,000 soldiers killed and captured, 2,400,000 gross tons of shipping sunk, 8,000 aircraft destroyed, 6,200 guns, and 2,550 tanks lost. Mr. Churchill flew back to England on June 5. He had made the outward journey by sea. The picture shows him leaving the battleship in which he had sailed.

German dams and power plants wrecked by R.A.F.

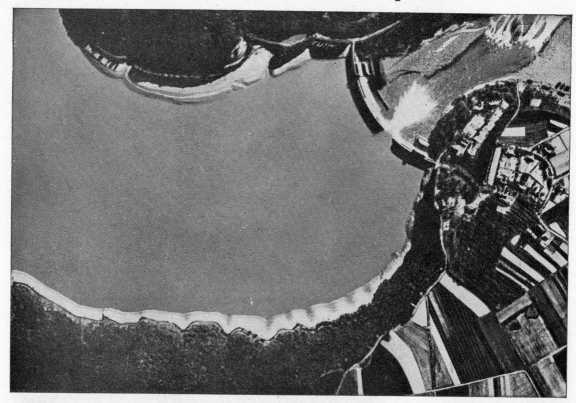

R.A.F. ATTACKS BIG GERMAN DAMS

On the nights of May 16-17, a force of Lancaster bombers, led by Wing-Commander G. P. Gibson, D.S.O., D.F.C., carried out an attack with mines on the great Eder and Mohne dams in German Westphalia. The Mohne dam was breached over a length of 100 yards, the power station being swept away by the resulting floods. The destruction of the Eder dam—the largest in Europe —set the Eder river below it in full flood. Later R.A.F. reconnaissance pilots reported great havoc as 134,000,000 tons of water swept down the Ruhr valley, wrecking factories, power stations, villages and railways. Eight bombers were lost. Pictures show: top, left, the breach left after the attack on the Eder dam; right, the breach in the Mohne dam; bottom, left, King George congratulating Commander Gibson after the raid.

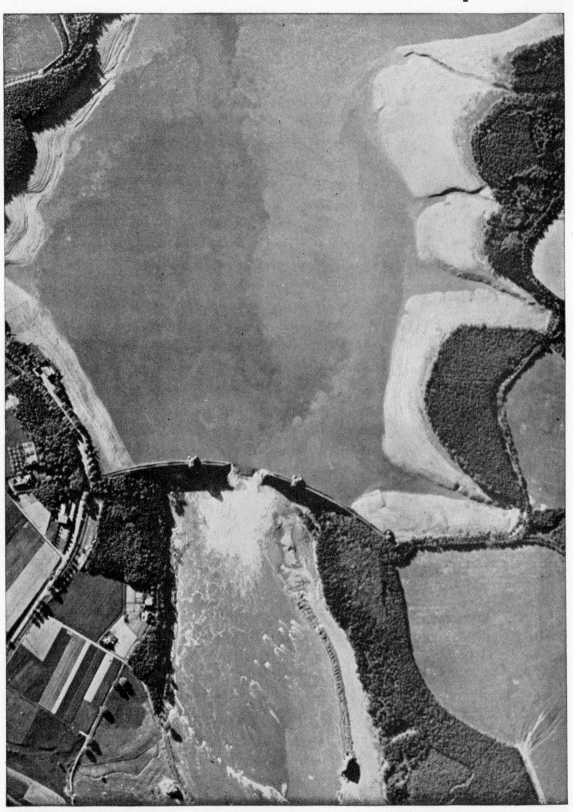

Strong American forces recapture Island of Attu

RECOVERY OF ALEUTIAN ISLANDS CONTINUES. Following the earlier occupation of Adak Island (Andreanof Group), U.S. forces in January landed unopposed on Amchitka Island and consolidated their positions there. A further stage in the clearing of the Japanese out of the Aleutians was reached on May 11, when American forces had landed on Attu, the outermost of the islands, which is 650 nautical miles east of the nearest Japanese-owned base and 196 miles west of Kiska, the other Aleutian island seized by the enemy in June, 1942. The Japanese had abandoned Attu the following September and reoccupied it in December. Under cover of a continuous bombardment from sea and air, the Americans poured a steady stream of reinforcements on to the island, and heavy fighting raged on the north coast around Holtz Bay. In spite of this the U.S. forces captured the high ground behind Holtz Bay, with what were reported to be slight casualties. On May 18 patrols from the American force advancing northwards from Massacre Bay joined up with the troops working inland from Holtz Bay. Later the same day the enemy withdrew to some high ground at the head of Chicagof harbor, where they attempted to make a stand, but by May 21

American official announcements were able to declare that the fighting had developed into a mopping-up process and that the alternatives facing the Japanese were surrender or liquidation. In spite of sleet, snow and rain, which tended to handicap operations, the American pressure increased and was reinforced by heavy bombardments from the sea, which, added to the continuous air strafing, totally reduced all buildings in the Chicagof area by May 26. At dawn on May 29 the Japanese launched a last desperate attack against the right wing of the U.S. forces in Chicagof valley and, with the exception of a few snipers, were completely annihilated. All organized enemy resistance thereupon collapsed. Two days later a broadcast from Washington said that small remaining pockets of resistance on Attu were being mopped up, and fewer than 200 Japanese were fighting back from machine-gun nests. Of the garrison which Tokio announced to consist of more than 2,000 men, 1,845 were later reported to have been killed. Only twenty were taken prisoner. The pictures show: left, part of the American landing force approaching Holtz Bay; and, right, men and equipment for the expeditionary force being put ashore at Massacre Bay.

The LST's do their part in the occupation of Attu

JAWS OF LST'S GAPE AT THE JAPS. In all parts of the Pacific where American fighting men have carried the battle to the foe—Attu, Rendova, Kiska, Munda and New Guinea—the gaping jaws of American landing craft (LST) have opened wide as though to swallow the foe. The designation means Landing

ship-tanks. Here marines are shown unloading the huge craft on Attu as a task force of the 7th Infantry Division took that base on the morning of May 11. Despite the mountainous character of the country the troops fought their way across the island to encircle the Japanese defending Chicagof Harbor.

British "Chindits" return to India from Burma

BRITISH GUERRILLA EXPEDITION IN BURMA. On May 20 a guerrilla force of British, Indian and Australian troops led by Brigadier O. C. Wingate, D.S.O., returned to India after a three-months' wrecking expedition behind the Japanese lines in the jungle of Central Burma. These highly trained men had crossed the Assam-Burma frontier on February 16, after which they operated in groups in the most difficult jungle and mountain country, penetrating more than 200 miles behind the enemy's lines. Frequently they went for many days without food or water and lived on whatever they could find till supplies could be dropped to them in the jungle clearings by parachute from British aircraft. They cut communication lines, destroyed bridges and supply dumps, and also killed hundreds of the enemy while suffering only light casualties themselves. The pictures show: left, supplies being dropped by parachute to the guerrillas in the jungle; and, above, Brigadier Wingate, who was killed early in 1944, talking to some of his men.

VICTORY CROWNS THE AFRICAN CAMPAIGN

By May 12 General Eisenhower was able to announce that organized resistance in all parts of Tunisia had ceased. He gave the highest praise to General Alexander for his strategy in the final offensive and for the manner in which he had deceived the enemy as to his intentions and accurately gauged how the enemy's mind would work. For 2,000 miles the Eighth Army had been the hammer and the First Army the anvil. Because of the efficiency and skill with which its long advance had been conducted, the Eighth Army had gained a well-deserved reputation as a fighting force, not only among the Allies, but in the minds of the enemy High Command as well. That the enemy's morale had snapped utterly was shown by a record which had been found of the German Commander-in-Chief's last signal. "I report," it read, "that the order to defend Tunisia to the last cartridge has been carried out." The operator who handled the signal had given the lie to this, however, by adding below: "Everything destroyed; we are now closing down." The Germans, in fact, surrendered in mass, whole divisions capitulating with their arms, equipment and food. One dump alone, found undamaged, contained 12,000 tons of ammunition. In addition to General von Arnim, the supreme Axis commander captured by British troops, enemy prisoners totalled more than 200,000, and vast quantities of abandoned enemy guns and war material fell into Allied hands. It was estimated that the enemy had suffered 30,000 casualties, killed and wounded. British casualties between April 17 and May 7 were 10,800 killed and wounded. In the final stages of the battle for Tunis, R.A.F. bombers flew 2,500 sorties in a day. Over an area of four miles by 1,000 yards scarcely a patch of surface escaped the rain of high explosives. In a message to General Eisenhower, King George expressed the country's heartfelt congratulations on the Allied victory. In the Tunisian capital on May 20 units from all the Allied forces marched through the town in celebration of the victorious conclusion of the long African campaign. All the Allied commanders were present, and the salute was taken by General Eisenhower, Alexander, Anderson and Giraud. The picture on these pages shows the Tunis victory parade in progress headed by a band of pipers of the 51st Highland Division.

CHINA ON THE OFFENSIVE
At the close of six years' resistance to Japanese
aggression, resourceful Chinese troops overcome all obstacles to surprise the enemy.

China's armies attack the Japanese invaders

DEFENDING GATEWAY TO CHUNGKING. The Japanese attack early in May, south of the Yangtze River, failed. Two strongly reinforced Japanese divisions were routed with heavy losses and Chinese troops captured an important pass leading to Chungking. At the end of May the Chinese launched an offensive near the Hupeh-Honan border, trapping five enemy divisions. Above, Chinese troops move up to the front; top, left, long lines of Chinese on the march; and bottom, left, camouflaged Chinese soldiers in the firing line.

Churchill and Allied military leaders confer in Algiers

WAR CONFERENCE AT ALGIERS

On May 27, after his visit to Washington, Mr. Churchill, accompanied by General Marshall, U.S. Army Chief of Staff, flew from the United States to Gibraltar. After passing one night there he proceeded to Allied Headquarters in North Africa and was joined in Algiers by Anthony Eden, who had flown from England. The Prime Minister had conversations with all the Allied leaders (among them Generals Eisenhower, Alexander, Anderson and Montgomery, Admiral Cunningham and Air Chief Marshal Tedder). He also met Generals Giraud and de Gaulle on June 4. Mr. Churchill visited the Tunisian battlefields and addressed 3,000 troops in the amphitheater in Carthage, near Tunis (picture, right). The other pictures show: top, members of the War Conference and, left, Mr. Churchill, General Montgomery and General Marshall.

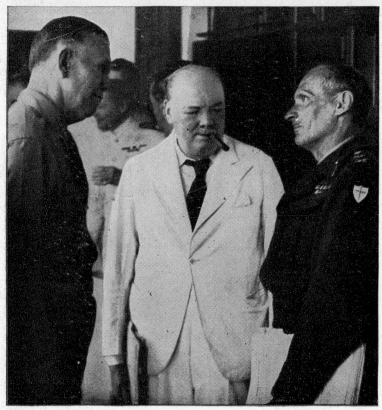

The meeting of Generals Giraud and de Gaulle at Algiers

DE GAULLE ARRIVES IN NORTH AFRICA. General de Gaulle, leader of the Fighting French since the fall of France in 1940, arrived in North Africa on May 30 for talks with General Giraud, Commander-in-Chief of the French forces in North Africa. This visit of General de Gaulle was the result of several months of negotiations between the French National Committee in London and General Giraud. The long-range exchange of views, effected through General Catroux, who had travelled to and from Britain with proposal

and counter-proposal, led eventually to General Giraud's agreement to a meeting at Algiers to discuss the co-ordination of Fighting French effort. The picture on the left shows the two leaders of Free French together. Their discussions culminated later in the establishment of the French Committee of National Liberation, presided over by the two Generals jointly. Meantime the French forces in North Africa, under General Giraud. were in action. Above, French troops are seen unloading mules on the way to the front.

ALLIES GAIN FOOTHOLD IN SOUTHERN EUROPE

After the Tunisian campaign came to an end and the Axis armies had been finally driven out of the African continent, the victorious Allies were soon in a position to make their next move in the Mediterranean war zone. The capture of the small, but strategically important, island of Pantelleria gave the British and U.S. air forces valuable advanced airfields to complement those of Malta and those along the North African shores. For any amphibious military operations against the Mediterranean coastline of Europe powerful support by fighter cover, or "air umbrella," was absolutely necessary. Indeed, as experience in this war had already shown, no landings on an enemy-occupied coast, however skilfully planned and boldly carried out, could hope to be successful without such fighter cover. The map on the right shows the approximate operational range of fighter aircraft based along the southern shores of the Mediterranean, including the islands of Malta and Pantelleria. It reveals, quite clearly, therefore, why Sicily (although it was known to be the most strongly defended of all the chief Italian islands) was selected for the initial attack on the "under belly" of Europe, instead of Sardinia or Corsica. As the map shows, Sicily lay well within operational range of Allied fighter aircraft, whereas Sardinia was only partly within their range and Corsica was right outside it. It follows, therefore, that while fighters could have accompanied military landings on Sardinia, they could not have covered such landings in anything approaching sufficient strength. Over Sicily, on the other hand, strong fighter protection could be provided quite easily. Another important factor which the Allied commanders must have undoubtedly had in mind when the decision to attack Sicily was made was its possession of a large number of first-class airfields which would prove of the greatest value for the next step in the Mediterranean campaign, the attack on the Italian mainland.

ROME
ADRIATIC
SEA
Velletri
Frosinone
Isernia
Campobasso
GULF OF
MANFREDONIA
Cassino
Foggia
I T A L Y
Barletta
Cerignola
Molfetta
BARI
GAETA
Corato
PONTINE
ISLANDS
Caserta
Benevento
Monopoli
Spinazzola
NAPLES
Avellino
Vesuvius
Altamura
BRINDISI
ISCHIA
Matera
CAPRI
SALERNO
Potenza
TARANTO
GULF OF SALERNO
Metaponto
Lecce
TENIAN
SEA
Otranto
GULF OF
TARANTO
Lauria
GULF OF
POLICASTRO
Castrovillari
Belvedere
Cariati
PROXIMATE OPERATIONAL RANGE OF FIGHTER AIRCRAFT
Paola
Cosenza
Amantea
Cotrone
Catanzaro
STROMBOLI
GULF OF
S. EUFEMIA
Pizzo
GULF OF
SQUILLACE
USTICA
Monasterace
LIPARI
ISLANDS
GULF OF GIOJA
Palmi
Castellammare
Milazzo
Scilla
Gerace
PALERMO
MESSINA
Reggio
Cefalu
C. Spartivento
TRAPANI
Termini
Taormina
Melito
Marsala
Mt. Etna
Giarre
Nicosia
S I C I L Y
Castelvetrano
CATANIA
Sciacca
Caltanissetta
Cape Corse
Gulf of St. Florent
Gerbini
Augusta
Calvi
Bastia
Gela
Caltagirone
Syracuse
Licata
Comiso
Corte
Cervione
Ragusa
CORSICA
Pachino
Gulf of Sagone
Cape Passero
Aleria
N
Solenzara
AJACCIO
E
Sartene
A
Strait of Bonifacio
GOZO
N
ASINARA
VALETTA
S
CAPRERA
LINOSA
E
Gulf of
Asinara
A
MALTA
Terranova
AMPIONE
LAMPEDUSA
SARDINIA

935

Allied air attacks bring about the surrender of Pantelleria

ALLIES CAPTURE PANTELLERIA. On June 11 the small Italian island of Pantelleria surrendered unconditionally. This immediately followed heavy day and night bombing and the shelling of enemy garrisons from the sea, after two previous Allied ultimatums, on June 9 and 10, had been rejected. One hour after the surrender, troops of the British First Division began to disembark on the island. After having overcome some slight resistance put up by Italian snipers they quickly gained their objectives. The island was occupied at a very small cost in Allied casualties, though a force of German dive bombers made a last-minute attempt to prevent the landings by bombing landing craft. These attacks were quite ineffective, as all the bombs fell wide. Pictures show: left, bombers over Pantelleria; top, right, shelling Pantelleria; above, the occupation.

Amphibs "show their teeth" as they dress for action

READY TO ADVANCE ON ENEMY SHORES—Lined up along the docks of a North African port, a flotilla of LST's (landing ship-tanks) ingest a mammoth menu of vehicles, supplies and men, which they will dis-

gorge on enemy shores. These LST's, a new departure in amphibious operations, played a prominent role
in the invasion of North Africa and were to play an even greater part in the campaign in Italy.

King George VI pays a visit to the African battlefront

THE KING FLIES TO THE FRONT

On June 12 a Service plane with two wing commanders at the controls landed on a North African airfield. Luggage in the plane was labelled T. Jerram, but out stepped the King, to be welcomed by General Eisenhower, Admiral Cunningham, and Air Chief Marshal Tedder. He had borrowed the name of Guardsman Jerram, his orderly, for his visit to the Eighth Army—the first time a King of England had ever flown to a battlefront. For several days he busied himself with consultations with service commanders, visits to the men of the forces, who welcomed him warmly, meetings with American military and naval leaders, and other activities. He spent a day with the Navy, shaking hands with many of the men who had seen action at Pantelleria, and talking to merchant sailors who had been engaged in hazardous convoy duty. With Sir Andrew Cunningham he visited units of the U.S. and British fleets in the Mediterranean, being piped aboard a British battleship and an American cruiser. The King inspected American infantry, watched a march past of armored forces, and exercises in street fighting. He invited General Giraud and General de Gaulle to lunch, with Robert Murphy, the American minister, and the British resident minister, Harold Macmillan. One of his visits, unofficial and unexpected, gave rise to a remarkable display of loyalty and enthusiasm. At a big convalescent rest centre by the sea, where several thousand soldiers were recuperating after wounds and illness, word flashed round that the King had arrived. Swiftly men raced to greet him, crowding, laughing, and cheering wildly, many of them dashing out of the water to be among the first to shake their visitor's hand. Suddenly somebody started the National Anthem. It was taken up with fervor and emotion, and when it had been finished the men cheered the King again and again. This picture shows the King walking between the packed lines of soldiers on the sands.

AIR BLITZ ON SICILY. Preparatory to invasion, the Allies flung their full air strength against Sicily, Sardinia, and the Italian mainland. In one period of twenty-four hours, concentrating upon Sicily, Allied bombers, strongly covered by fighters based on Malta, destroyed several hundred planes on Sicilian airfields and shot down forty-four enemy planes in the air for an Allied loss of thirteen. The airfields of Catania, Gerbini, Sciacca, Comiso, and Milo were heavily attacked. Above, Martin "Marauders" bomb an airfield.

CATANIA ATTACKED FROM THE AIR. Both before and during the invasion the large port and airfield of Catania were heavily bombed again and again, and enormous damage was done to the harbor and other important military targets. Though these raids often met with opposition, they provided significant evidence that the savage power of the Luftwaffe was weakening, for among the many types of Axis planes shot down, many would not have been used but for shortage of aircraft. Above, fires in Catania after a raid.

RENDOVA OCCUPIED. On June 30 U.S. Marines landed on Rendova, a mountainous island in the New Georgia group, 170 miles north-west of Guadalcanal. Enemy opposition was quickly overcome and within a few hours the whole island was occupied. Rendova is separated by only a seven-mile strait from New Georgia Island, where the Japanese held Munda and its important airfield. The picture above shows the Americans landing on Rendova. Those opposite: top, Australian troops at Sanananda, New Guinea; and bottom, Japanese prisoners captured by Americans in the Guadalcanal campaign.

Americans take Japanese by surprise on Rendova Island

AIR COVERAGE. Flying at tree top height, a U.S. Army P-40 snarls over a group of American infantry men charging across the beach at Rendova, in the Central Solomons. The Allied attack caught the Japanese by surprise and aerial opposition was small in the early hours of the attack. Thousands of picked

troops came ashore under their fleet guns and the greatest plane concentration of the Solomons campaign, which took the American forces farther along in the direction of Tokio. Southerners joined Northerners in a battle song "Marching through New Georgia," as landing craft snaked through tortuous reefs.

How Rendova Island looked to Marine eyes on invasion day

BRINGING THE MARINES ASHORE. Swift landing craft pour American forces ashore at Rendova Island as Army and Marine units closed in on the Japanese air base at Munda, eight miles away. From Rendova artillery rained fire on the Japanese field, which soon fell to American land forces. The all-out assault

on this Japanese stronghold of New Georgia got under way at dawn. The brilliantly conceived and daringly executed plan caught the foe flat-footed; the landing of men and materials had actually begun before the enemy shore batteries opened fire, but by that time the ships had landed every man.

A member of a Nazi wolf pack gets a "going-over"

A NAVY PLANE SCORES A HIT. Riding in a U.S. Navy plane, a Navy photographer got this remarkable close-up of a direct hit on a U-boat which was attempting to waylay a convoy in the North Atlantic. One

bare-legged Nazi stands in awe of the monumental column of spray as another ducks. A depth bomb can be seen (arrow) about to hit the water in an attempt to deliver a coup de grace to the raider.

Allies continue the Mediterranean offensive

ALLIED INVASION OF SICILY

At 10 o'clock on Friday night, July 9, gliders packed with Allied troops dropped behind the enemy lines in Sicily, and the invasion of the island had begun. The gliders were quickly followed by paratroops, and through the next two days American and British landing forces made contact with the air borne units, breached the coastal defenses, and established bridgeheads at many selected points. Protected by a great fleet of Allied warships, and by the Allied Air Forces, which had secured air supremacy, mighty reinforcements of men, tanks, guns, equipment, and supplies were successfully landed. Enemy coastal batteries were put out of action by the guns of the Fleet. By July 11 the first immediate objectives had been taken, and three Sicilian airfields were in Allied hands. One of these was at Pachino, captured by British and Canadian assault troops. American forces occupied two airfields at Gela, where the enemy, supported by tanks, made a counter-attack, which was successfully beaten off. Axis forces opposing the invasion were estimated at 400,000, including 100,000 Italians. The German radio admitted that the first phase of the attack had been successful at several points, and an Italian commentator boasted that the Allies would "bite their teeth out" on the strong Italian fortifications. The picture shows one of the many Sicilian landings.

SICILY INVADED
By landing in Sicily on 10 July, 1943, Allied troops
regained a foothold in Europe for the first time since
the collapse of France and the retreat from Dunkirk

ZERO HOUR FOR INVASION ARMADA. Under the command of Admiral of the Fleet Sir Andrew Cunningham, 3,266 surface ships were engaged in the invasion of Sicily. This mighty armada of the Allies comprised craft of every type, from battleships to L.S.T.'s. In spite of adverse changes in the weather, of rising wind and choppy seas, the convoys of this multitude of ships made their crossings with such precision that the Allied landings on the beaches were carried out exactly to timetable. From long before dawn flare after flare arose from beach after beach at the appointed zero hour to signal "landing successful," and thereafter all the supplies, arms, and equipment of the invading armies streamed steadily ashore. These pictures show: top, a landing party coming ashore, and below, the British safely land a Bren carrier.

BRITISH AND CANADIANS JOIN HANDS. One of the early successes of the invasion was the determined capture of the Pachino peninsula by British and Canadian assault troops, who landed on Costa dell Ambra beach, four miles from Pachino. They established a bridgehead within twenty-four hours, and then advanced inland to start the hard-fought campaign which was to end in the conquest of Sicily.

Novel amphibious trucks keep Allied armies supplied

FIRST WEEK OF SICILIAN INVASION

At dawn on Saturday, July 10, the first assault troops landed on the Sicily beaches, and the success of the greatest amphibian operation in history was quickly proved. Before seven o'clock that morning all landings were established; Allied infantry were advancing into the interior; a few hours later the harbor of Syracuse was captured. British forces landed east of Cape Passero, Canadians on the western side, while United States forces came ashore at Gela. On the next day the Canadians took Pachino, and its airfield was very soon in use by Allied aircraft. On Tuesday, the 13th, American forces captured Comiso and its airfield, joined up with the Canadians, and commanded the railway from Syracuse to Ragusa. By the next day seven of Sicily's airfields were firmly in the hands of the Allies. The Eighth Army successfully repelled fierce German counter-attacks. During Thursday and Friday the Eighth Army fought desperately for Lentini. The Americans and Canadians advanced and captured half a dozen towns. Lentini was occupied on Saturday, July 17. Pictures show the amphibious DUKWS (known as "Ducks"), which were used with success in the landing operations. This six-wheeled truck has a motor engine which drives wheels on land and a propeller at sea. Top, "Ducks" approaching shore; bottom, left, drawing away from a ship; right, returning for another load

LEADERS OF THE ARMIES. Studying a map of Sicily at the Royal Palace in Palermo, are, left to right,
Major General Geoffrey Keyes, General Sir Bernard L. Montgomery and Lieut. General George S. Patton,
Jr., commander of the American 7th Army.General Patton later made an excellent record for himself in
the Sicilian campaign. This was marred to some extent by an unfortunate incident, the news of which was
not released by the Army until months loter. During an inspection of one of the field hospitals near the
front line, General Patton struck an invalided soldier who was obviously suffering from combat hysteria.
The General later made a profuse public apology and the affair was attributed to the tension of battle.
After Sicily General Patton was relieved of command of the 7th Army to assume a high post in London.

FIRST SICILY WOUNDED AWAIT EMBARKATION. Stretcher cases, wounded at Syracuse, waiting in landing craft to go aboard a hospital ship. On the first day of the invasion the hospital ship Talamba, was sunk by the enemy, although the vessel was fully lighted in accordance with the Geneva convention.

Americans and British make progress in Sicily

EIGHTH ARMY'S THRUST FOR CATANIA. Within five days of the initial landings remarkable progress was achieved by the Allied forces. The U.S. Seventh Army under General Patton, which had encountered strong enemy opposition, not only held firmly to the bridgeheads at Licata and Gela, but even enlarged them. New Allied landings were made near Catania, which was the goal of the British Eighth Army under General Montgomery. Canadian units of his command joined up with the Americans at Ragusa, twenty miles inland, and Allied cruisers and monitors bombarded Augusta and entered the port on July 13, a party from H.M.S. Exmoor hoisting the white ensign over the town. On July 15 the British advanced to Bruccoli, less than twenty miles from Catania. Four Italian generals were killed in action, and another surrendered

with all his staff. Seven airfields were securely in Allied possession, and prisoners taken in Sicily totalled 12,000. One of the airfields—Ponte Olivo—was taken by a fierce bayonet attack. German attempts to bring reinforcements into the struggle were frustrated by heavy air attacks upon vital links of communication, Turin being heavily bombed by Lancasters which flew across France and returned by the Atlantic. This was the third big successive campaign for the British Eighth, the other two being Libya and Tunisia. Pictures show: top, left, troops of the 78th Division mopping up in a captured town; centre, enemy gun captured at Syracuse in firing order; right, Canadian miners at work; bottom, left, British infantry rounding up snipers near Augusta; right, civilians giving a welcome to British troops at Pachino.

THE CAMPAIGN IN SICILY

The Allied attack on Sicily began with massed airborne and naval landings in the south-east corner of the island on July 10 and virtually ended with the fall of Messina on August 17. The island was finally occupied after only six weeks of hard fighting by U. S. British and Canadian troops. They were delayed in their progress by the rugged and mountainous territory, by the difficulties of maintaining supplies and communications, and, not least, by the determined resistance of the German divisions, especially in the Plain of Catania. After the initial landings in the extreme south, the Allies soon gained their primary objectives, including many good airfields and the great port of Syracuse. Actually the enemy was taken completely by surprise, for, having expected the main Allied landings from the direction of Bizerte and other North-West African ports, they concentrated their main defenses in the north-west corner of Sicily. What the Allies did, however, was to land a large part of their forces from Malta, where, on account of the shorter sea crossing, the landings could be made under the cover of massed fighter aircraft. After the main bridgeheads had been established along a coastline of roughly one hundred miles, the Allies fanned out as they proceeded to advance rapidly inland. The Americans drove westwards along the coast, captured Agrigento, and then advanced to Palermo, the occupation of which cut off thousands of Italian troops in the north-west corner. The Canadians captured Ragusa, then fought their way through to the center of the island to take the important key towns of Enna and Leonforte. Meanwhile the Eighth Army advanced from Syracuse and Augusta towards the Catania Plain. It was here that the Germans made their greatest stand. The Eighth Army's break-through towards Randazzo and Messina was thus delayed until U. S. and Canadian troops were able to sweep down from the north coast and smash the German rear.

ALLIED LANDINGS, JULY 10
ALLIED ADVANCE, JULY 13
" JULY 16
" JULY 19
" JULY 22
" JULY 28
" AUG. 14
AERODROMES   NAVAL BASES
MILES 0   10   20   30   40   50

S.J.TURNER, F.R.G.S.

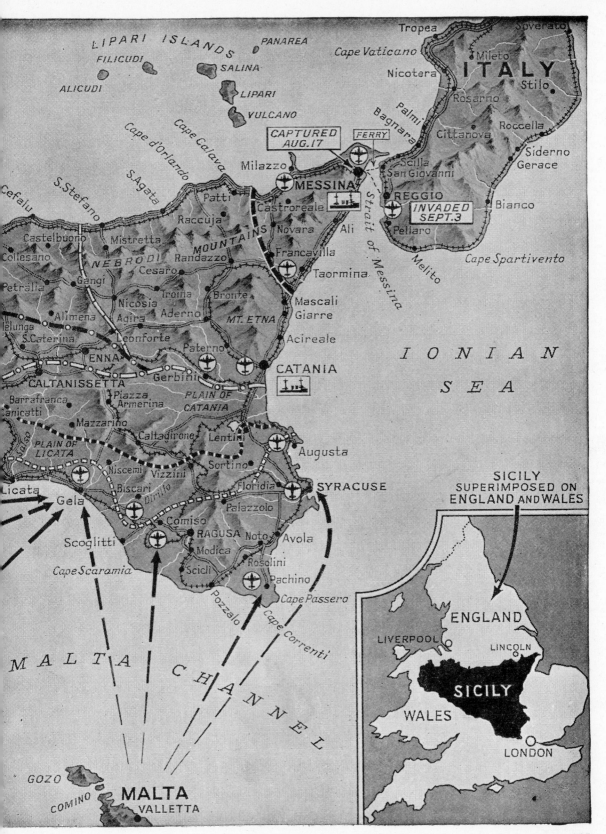

LIPARI ISLANDS
PANAREA
FILICUDI
SALINA
ALICUDI
LIPARI
VULCANO

Cape d'Orlando
Cape Calava

Tropea
Soverato
Cape Vaticano
Mileto
Nicotera
ITALY
Stilo
Rosarno
Roccella
Bagnara
Palmi
Cittanova
Siderno
Gerace
Scilla
San Giovanni
REGGIO
Bianco
INVADED
SEPT. 3
Pellaro
Melito
Cape Spartivento

CAPTURED
AUG. 17
FERRY
MESSINA
Milazzo
Strait of Messina

Patti
Castroreale
S.Stefano
S.Agata
Novara
Ali
S.Agata
Raccuja
Francavilla
Cefalu
Castelbuono
Mistretta
MOUNTAINS
Taormina
Collesano
NEBRODI
Randazzo
Cesaro
Mascali
Petralia
Gangi
Troina
Bronte
Giarre
Nicosia
Aderno
Acireale
lelunga
Adira
MT. ETNA
S.Caterina
Leonforte
ENNA
Paterno
IONIAN
CALTANISSETTA
Gerbini
SEA
Barrafranca
Piazza
PLAIN OF
anicatti
Armerina
CATANIA
CATANIA
Mazzarino
Caltagirone
Lentini
PLAIN OF
Augusta
LICATA
Niscemi
Vizzini
Sortino
Salso
Biscari
Dirillo
Floridia
SYRACUSE
Licata
Palazzolo
Gela
Comiso
Noto
SICILY
Scoglitti
RAGUSA
Avola
SUPERIMPOSED ON
Modica
Rosolini
ENGLAND AND WALES
Cape Scaramia
Scicli
Pachino
Cape Passero
Pozzallo
Cape Correnti
ENGLAND
LIVERPOOL
LINCOLN
M A L T A   C H A N N E L
SICILY
WALES
GOZO
LONDON
COMINO
MALTA
VALLETTA

The Allies lose a ship in the invasion of Sicily

GOING UP IN SMOKE. An Allied ship, part of a convoy carrying supplies to the invasion forces at Gela, Sicily, explodes after a direct hit from Nazi planes just outside the harbor of this Sicilian town. The difficulties of maintaining supplies for the invading American and British troops was one of the

major obstacles to this six-week campaign. Fortunately for the Allies, complete control of the sea lanes was in their hands. The Italian Navy had long since ceased to be a factor, and the Mediterranean was being patrolled by Allied warships exclusively, with the exception of a few Axis submarines.

Death of an American fighting ship in the Sicilian invasion

FAREWELL TO A HONORED SHIP. A bright blur of flame marks the end of the LCI-1, a landing craft (infantry) which had been honored by a Presidential citation for the part she played in the Sicilian

invasion. The ship went down during an Axis raid on Allied shipping in Sicilian waters. Over her burning hull an arch of anti-aircraft fire is raised as though in homage to the ship and her men.

A stepping stone on the road to Italy and victory

SICILIAN LANDING. Vari-sized American landing craft line the shore at Scoglitti, Sicily, as Allied troops land on the island—en route to Italy. The U. S. Army's amphibious "ducks" and the Navy's LCI's (Landing craft-Infantry), LCM's (Landing craft-mechanized), LCT's (Landing craft-tanks) and LCVR's

(Landing craft-personnel ramp) join in the mammoth operation. Scoglitti, located on the southwest tip of Sicily, was one of ten towns captured that day, giving complete control of this section to American troops. The capture of Scoglitti was a stepping stone to the taking of the important town of Agrigento.

American methods on a beachhead in Sicily

RACE AGAINST TIME IN SICILY. Working coolly and methodically despite the constant danger of enemy attack, U. S. troops build a road with steel matting over the sandy Sicilian shore during landing operations near Scoglitti. Outlined against the far horizon, the ships of the vast invasion armada hover

like protecting floating fortresses, their guns ever ready to lay down a curtain of fire. These operations in the Scoglitti sector were extremely important and served as preliminary moves to the occupation of the west coast and the final pincer movement in cooperation with the British Army on the east coast.

Germans fortify Crete against British attacks

GERMAN FEARS OF INVASION. The Allied victories in North Africa represented, in the words of Winston Churchill, an immediate threat to the "soft under-belly of Europe" and the occupying German and Italian forces on the island of Crete reacted in characteristic fashion to the danger. A British commando raid on airfields and installations in Crete on the night of July 3-4. was followed by savage reprisals against the civilian population, accused by the Nazis of connivance in the raid. The picture, top, left, gives some idea of the cold-bloodedness in which these barbarous atrocities were committed. The other pictures show strong Nazi-built fortifications in Axis-occupied Crete.

Germans launch a summer offensive in Russia

FRESH GERMAN ATTACK IN RUSSIA FAILS. On July 5 an intensive enemy artillery and aerial bombardment broke the comparitive lull which had continued on the Russian front since the spring thaws had brought large-scale operations to a standstill. Large German tank and infantry forces with strong air cover launched the expected enemy summer offensive on a 200-mile front in the Orel-Byelgorod sector. The battle that ensued developed into some of the bitterest fighting of the war, with both sides throw-

ing in masses of armor and infantry. But in spite of minor breaches of their positions here and there, made at enormous cost to the enemy, the Russians, by their stubborn resistance, completely neutralized the German attempt to repeat their massed drive to the East in the previous summer. By July 14 the enemy attacks had dwindled and, indeed, the Germans had again been forced back to their original positions. The photograph shows Red Army troops attacking an enemy strong point in a Russian village near Orel.

The Red army hits back in drive towards Orel

RUSSIAN SUMMER OFFENSIVE BEGINS. On July 12, after the failure of the recent German assault on their positions, the Red Army launched a powerful offensive on a twenty-five mile front to the north and east of Orel. Within three days the enemy's fortifications had been pierced to a depth of twenty-eight miles and three German infantry divisions and two Panzer divisions utterly routed. On July 17 the Red Army began their mighty attack on the Orel-Kursk-Byelgorod sector, and it was soon apparent that, not only had the German plan of a summer offensive, as Marshal Stalin announced, been "completely frustrated," but, in fact, the Russians had achieved a victory of the first magnitude. The Red Army eliminated all the wedges that had been driven into their positions in the abortive German offensive. The pictures on these pages show: above Red Army tanks taking up their fighting stations before the Russian offensive began; top, right, German infantry in retreat use every kind of transport to escape encirclement or annihilation; bottom, right, German soldiers firing a Russian village as they retreat.

The Red army advances across the Upper Don

FIERCE FIGHTING BEFORE OREL. During the remainder of July fighting continued on a big scale in the Orel sector. Despite heavy rains and strong German Resistance the Red Army advanced steadily, and by August 1 they had reached places within twelve miles of the city. The picture on these pages show Red Army cavalry in action. The Cossacks, especially, played a great part in the Don and Caucasus fighting earlier in the year. Left, Cossack warriors riding into battle; above, Red troops crossing a river.

The Russian armies retake Orel and Byelgorod

RUSSIANS WIN GREAT DOUBLE VICTORY. On August 5 Moscow radio announced the recapture of Orel and Byelgorod exactly one month after the Germans began their unsuccessful offensive on this front. Orel, which had been in German hands for nearly two years, was one of the chief enemy bases in Russia during that time. While the fighting for Orel and Byelgorod lasted, the Red Army inflicted severe losses on their enemy, losses that would surely have serious repercussions on morale in the German

forces. Between July 5 and August 5 the German losses were 100,000 killed and 4,600 tanks, 1,623 guns, 11,000 trucks and 2,500 aircraft, while in the same period the Red Army captured 521 tanks, 875 guns, 2,521 machine guns, 325 supply dumps and 12,400 prisoners. Yet on the eve of the offensive Hitler himself had issued an order of the day, declaring that that attack would be "the turning-point of the war and the last battle for Germany's victory." Picture shows a Russian farmer returning to her ruined homestead.

ARCHITECT OF FASCISM OVERTHROWN

As the Allied forces pressed north in Sicily and came within sight of the Italian mainland, Mussolini, first Fascist dictator, found himself facing internal revolt, which increasingly revealed itself in strikes and sabotage. So serious was the situation on both the war and the home fronts that he went to consult Hitler, who met him at Verona on July 19. Hitler's proposed remedies were reported by Mussolini to the Fascist Grand Council, specially summoned to Rome on July 24. But the writing was already on the wall for this "sawdust Cæsar"; a majority of the Council rejected his proposals, and the cornered and frantic Duce was forced to resign. To the people of Italy the tidings came like the sweet breath of Freedom, unsavored for twenty-one weary years, and in the cities and towns the jubilant crowds demonstrated in the streets for days. To all outside Italy, particularly the millions suffering under Nazi oppression, the fall of Mussolini brought new confidence that his master across the Alps would meet the same fate. Pictures on this page show: top, what the citizens of a Sicilian town did to one of his innumerable effigies; below, the effacing of one of the slogans he had caused to be painted on public buildings all over Italy. This one reads: "Great Britain has finally felt deeply the bite of the Roman wolf." On the oppsite page an Italian crowd is shown hurling overripe fruit at another of Mussolini's portraits.

American daylight raid on Rumanian oilfields

AMERICAN AIRCRAFT SHATTER RUMANIAN OILFIELDS. Ploesti and its famous oilfields, covering an area of nineteen square miles, were bombed for the fourth time on August 1. Nearly 200 Liberators and 2,000 specially-trained airmen took part in this very heavy attack on a target of vital importance to the enemy—it was estimated that Ploesti, thirty-five miles from Bucharest, supplied one-third of all the oil fuel Germany required for war purposes. This mass raid involved a round journey of 2,400 miles. It was carried out at low level, many of the aircraft attacking from 500 feet and under, to insure accurate placing of their bombs. They smashed down 270 tons of high-explosives upon the thirteen oil refineries, the pumping stations, and the storage tanks, causing huge explosions and devastating damage. Many of the installations were put out of action. Much of the destruction was done by delayed-action bombs. Above, one of the attacking aircraft sweeps in just over the smoke-stacks, against a background of smoke and flame. Top, right: Liberators streaking into the attack through a gap in the dense smoke clouds; below, one of the storage tanks going up in flames during the first moments of the raid.

EIGHTH ARMY IN AUGUSTA. Troops of the Eighth Army occupied the Italian naval and seaplane base of Augusta after it had been repeatedly bombed by the R.A.F. and shelled by the Allied Fleet. The first ship to enter the harbor was the Greek destroyer Kanaris, which engaged the shore batteries as she steamed in. Not only during the landings, but throughout the course of the Sicilian expedition, the Allied navies played a great part in supporting the land forces, subjecting Sicily to fifty organized bombardments. Above, British troops in Augusta, as smoke pours out of a shelled building.

CAPTURE OF CATANIA. Early on August 5 troops of the Eighth Army entered Catania. The people of the city welcomed the men of the victorious army with extraordinary enthusiasm. They clapped and shouted: "Viva!", they seized the soldiers' hands to shake them, they danced down the bomb-shattered streets by the side of the marching men. And they begged for food. The fall of Centuripe, a mountain stronghold with ridge on ridge held by snipers, which General Patton's 78th Division had captured, had made the fall of Catania certain. Above: British troops passing through one of the bombed streets.

Looting in Catania after the German retreat

RIOTS BEFORE THE ALLIES TAKE CATANIA

General Montgomery's personal message to the troops on August 1 made it clear that a new Allied offensive in Sicily had begun. "Let us get on with the job," said General Montgomery. "Together with our American Allies, we knocked Mussolini off his perch. We will now drive the Germans from Sicily. Into battle with stout hearts. Good luck to you all." After brilliant successes in the opening stages of the Sicilian campaign, the advance of Eighth Army had been halted by the enemy's formidable line of defenses along the Simeto river. The strongest bastions of that line were at Regalbuto and Centuripe. After much hard fighting the Eighth Army succeeded in occupying the mountains dominating the Simeto valley. The Canadians occupied Regalbuto, and the Americans captured Troina and Capizzi. Prime Minister Churchill promptly informed the House of Commons of their successes: "Our general offensive in Sicily began to develop on Sunday afternoon (August 1), and all Monday was passed in full battle. Large reinforcements have been moved up to the fighting front, and it has been properly garnished with artillery and supplies of every kind." The 78th Division won a notable victory by storming the fortress-like position of Centuripe. The success compelled the Germans to begin the evacuation of Catania, enabling Allied forces to enter the Catanian plain. On August 5 Catania surrendered to the British Army. Picture shows Italians looting buildings in Catania.

The conquest of Sicily almost complete

FALL OF TAORMINA. On August 16 Eighth Army troops captured Taormina. The Germans fought stubbornly in rearguard actions, but enemy evacuation was steadily going on. Enemy troops were escaping over the Straits of Messina, at the rate of a thousand a day, while the R.A.F. kept up an almost ceaseless attack on the beaches, and on the ferries, barges and lighters crammed with beaten fugitives. Messina,

which had been the target of many attacks by the R.A.F. and U.S.A.A.F., was again heavily bombed. Pictures: top, the Bishop self-propelled gun-tank combination, which did much effective work in the mountainous Sicilian country; bottom, left, British patrol passing the dead bodies of Italians in a street of Avola, right, wrecked German troop-carrying tractor rests in a bomb crater on Messina waterfront.

BRITISH GUNS COVER THE FINAL ASSAULT
ON THE ENEMY IN SICILY

SICILY CONQUERED

After the fall of Catania on August 5, British and Canadian forces pressed forward and made important gains north of Regalbuto. The Eighth Army pressed northward along the coast road to Messina, fifty miles away. Ships of the Allied fleets kept up a heavy bombardment of Messina. The Germans made every effort to delay the advance of the Allies by mines and large scale demolitions, but numbers of Germans and Italians were already assembling on the beaches of Messina preparatory to evacuation, and evacuation barges were being pounded and sunk by Allied planes. The Allies remained master of the air. According to R.A.F. calculations, 12,000 German and Italian aircraft had been destroyed in the Middle East and North African campaigns since the entrance of Italy into the war. In Sicily alone, up to the surrender of Catania, the number of Axis prisoners was 100,000. On August 10 the Eighth Army and the U. S. Seventh Army linked up between Troina and Randazzo, and on the 17th the honor of capturing Messina fell to the Americans. All organized resistance on the island ceased. After a campaign of thirty-nine days the Sicilian campaign was over. Up to August 10 Axis losses were 167,000— 32,000 killed or wounded and 135,000 prisoners. Allied casualties were 25,000 killed, wounded, and taken prisoner. The picture shows American troops entering Messina on August 17.

Nazis fail to subdue determined Yugoslav patriots

YUGOSLAV GUERRILLAS HARRY THE ENEMY. Patriot forces opposing the enemy occupying armies in Yugoslavia intensified their resistance over still wider objectives, and the Yugoslav Government G.H.Q. in Cairo reported on August 28 a number of recent successes. These included a daring attack on the Rajlovac (Serajevo) airfield on August 10 and the consequent destruction of twenty-eight German aircraft; the ambushing of a German armored train near Serajevo; the capture of three towns, including an important coal-mining center, in Bosnia and Slovenia; also the cutting at numerous places of the railway line in Dalmatia and the wrecking of key bridges. Some idea of the heroism behind the blows which the partisans were striking came from the enemy in this series of pictures showing: above, a lamp-post hanging of a patriot by the Germans in Belgrade; top, right, guerrillas captured by German troops; and, below, a band of captured guerrillas being marched away to face a Nazi firing squad.

MAMMOTH HARVEST
Biggest crops in Britain's history were safely gathered to time by U.S. Army volunteers and by workers on holiday.

Nazis force peasants to bring in the Ukraine harvest for Germans

NAZIS STEAL UKRAINE HARVEST. German spokesmen declared on more than one occasion that the German people would not go short of food, whatever might be the plight of the inhabitants in the countries Germany had overrun. The Nazis carried out systematic and ruthless pillage of the resources of the occupied countries. They forced whole populations of Russian villages into slave labor, compelling them to help gather the harvests of the Ukraine, and sending the full yield to Germany. Vast agricultural tracts in the rich Ukraine passed into their possession. When the brilliant successes of the Red Army in the summer campaign of 1943 forced the Germans to retreat, the latter made every effort to secure the harvest for their own use. It is estimated that they obtained from the Ukraine nearly half a million tons of grain for the needs of their invading armies. They deported numbers of the Russian population to

Germany. After the Russian reoccupation of the Ukraine, there were many atrocity stories, confirmed and unconfirmed, told by the surviving peasant population. In several instances the guilt was actually pinned on captured German officers who were tried, convicted and executed for these offenses. Top, Nazi guns on fields during harvest; bottom, left, Russians forced to work under German guard; right, Nazi soldiers speed up the work of harvesting and dispatch the cream of the crop home to Germany.

German capital undergoes intensive aerial bombardment

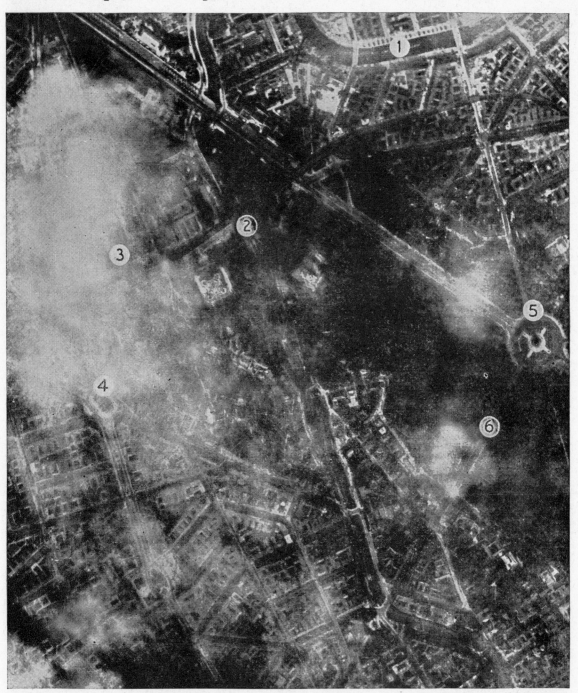

SMASHING AIR ATTACK ON BERLIN. Bomber Command of the R.A.F. smashed Berlin on August 23 in the heaviest and most concentrated attack the capital of Germany had ever experienced. Seven hundred planes took part. In fifty minutes they dropped 1,700 tons of bombs, causing enormous devastation. Great fires were still burning at the end of the next day, and reconnaissance aircraft reported vast clouds of smoke four miles high. Important electrical works and plants were badly damaged, and railway stations were wrecked. Above, a reconnaissance photograph which reveals 100 fires still burning and shows distinctive features of the city: 1, River Spree; 2, two "flak" towers; 3, Zoo station; 4, Augusta Victoria Platz; 5, Grosse Stern; 6, Tiergarten. Top, right, women leaving the city; below, women sleeping out.

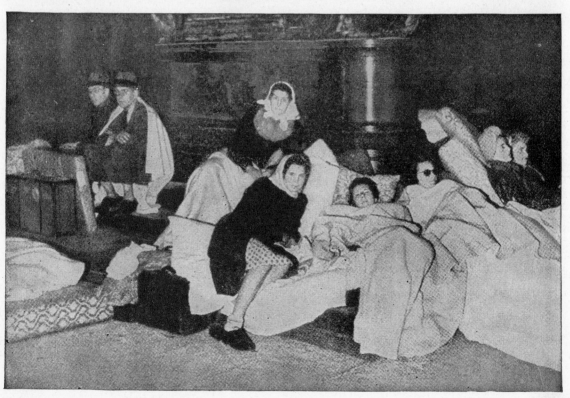

The people of Berlin get a taste of their own medicine

THE BATTLE OF BERLIN. In just over a week after the big attack with 1,700 tons of bombs, a great force of R.A.F. bombers carried out on August 31 another devastating onslaught on Berlin. This time the attack lasted forty-five minutes, and 1,000 tons of high-explosive and incendiary bombs were dropped. Forty-seven British planes were lost. Numbers of the German night fighters were shot down by the bombers.

Pictures show scenes in the city and outskirts on the days following the raid by the R.A.F.; left, Berliners having a meal in the open air, with a large burned-out building in the background; top, right, bombed-out people living in the woods outside the city where light wooden shacks were hurriedly put together to shelter citizens whose houses had been destroyed; bottom, right, an emergency kitchen in the capital.

Russian thrusts towards Bryansk and Kharkov

NEW SUCCESSES BY RED ARMY. The Russians followed up their success at Orel and Byelgorod with with a six-mile advance on August 6 when they reoccupied over seventy inhabited places. On both the Bryansk and Kharkov fronts the Germans were driven back in hopeless disorder as the Russian advances gained momentum. On August 12, after defeating strong enemy counter-attacks, the Red Army recaptured Chuguyev, an important German base twenty miles south-east of Kharkov, and two days later bitter street fighting was raging in the northern suburbs of the city. The victory at Chuguyev was swiftly suc-

ceeded by fresh advances on the Bryansk front, where the Russians liberated yet another sixty localities including the towns of Aktinino and Novlya, a junction of the Bryansk-Kharkov and the Bryansk-Konotop railways. For several days the enemy launched one counter-attack after another, throwing in huge tank an infantry forces, and although their fury temporarily held up the Red Army they were all repulsed. With losses estimated at 4,000 men a day the Germans began to show signs of exhaustion. Meanwhile, they were subjected to heavy air blows. Picture shows Russian infantrymen chasing the enemy.

The Red army again liberates Kharkov

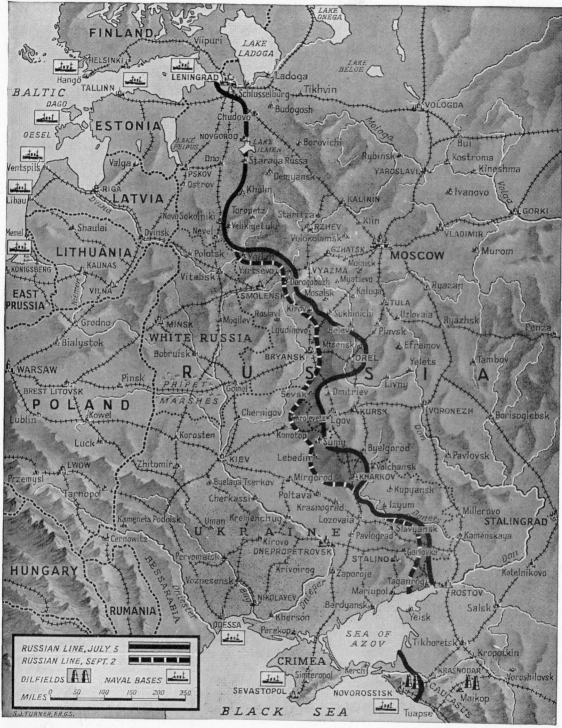

RED ARMY RECAPTURES KHARKOV. During the course of the war between Russia and Germany, Kharkov, the second largest city of the Soviet Union, had been four times captured. Twice the inhabitants of the city had known the bitterness of subjection to the German invaders. After retaking Rostov in February, the Red Army had delivered Kharkov. But they had been unable to hold the city. On March 15 the Germans again entered Kharkov, and made it one of the most important bastions of the summer

campaign. They strove hard to keep the city, but despite all their efforts the Russians attacked desperately time and again, pressing their attacks on three sides with such success that eventually they had all but ringed the city, leaving the enemy the use of only one railway. Thus they forced the Germans to evacuate Kharkov and to retreat, and on August 23 the city was liberated. The map, left, shows limit of Russian summer advance. Top, right, Germans retreat from Orel; below, a bridge blown up by the enemy.

GERMANS RETREAT ALONG WHOLE RUSSIAN FRONT. During the last days of August the Red Army improved its positions along a vast front from the Smolensk area to the Sea of Azov. Progress was especially good on the Kharkov front where, on August 27, the Russians reoccupied Kotelva, sixty miles west of Kharkov. Meanwhile, our victorious Allies pressed on to Taganrog, the important Sea of Azov port. Pictures show: left, a German outside a blazing farmstead; above, a Russian family returns home.

Allied pressure increases in the North and South Pacific

ALLIES ADVANCE IN THE PACIFIC. After landings which began on August 15, the island of Kiska in the North Pacific was retaken by United States and Canadian forces. The loss of Attu by the Japanese had jeopardized the enemy's supply lines and rendered enemy positions on Kiska hazardous, and Japanese troops evacuated the island under cover of fog. Far South, in the South-West Pacific, the Allies made good progress in New Guinea, employing their superiority in the air to smash the important air-

fields of Lae so thoroughly that the Japanese were unable to make use of them for any effective retalia-
tion. This terrific "softening" of Lae was carried out systematically by U.S. heavy bombers, Liberators
and Fortresses, in preparation for invasion. The Allies were determined to secure the great advantages
of the harbor and airfields of Lae. Left, bombs bursting on a Jap airfield at Lae; right, top, United States
troops land on Kiska Island; below, two midget submarines abandoned by the Japanese.

LAUNCHING ATTACK ON KISKA. Members of the joint American-Canadian force look over the rail of their landing craft toward comrades climbing the barren slopes contiguous to the harbor in which the attack was launched against Kiska at dawn, only to discover that the Japanese had fled under cover of fog.

AMPHIBIOUS OPERATIONS. An LST (Landing Ship, Tanks) with open bow doors, is shown in operation during the invasion of Kiska in this photograph by a U.S. Coast Guard officer whose ship participated
in the unopposed occupation of this important Japanese-held base in the Aleutian Islands.

Coast Guardsmen participate in invasion operations in Aleutians

COMING ASHORE AT KISKA. The bow doors of two LSTs that have disgorged their cargoes of men and equipment yawn open at Kiska. Hitherto a secret, this photograph by a United States Coast Guard officer was among the first to be released showing the open bow doors of LSTs (Landing ship, tanks).

The opening bow doors are probably the most revolutionary development in amphibious operations in modern warfare. The ships were so constructed that they could practically land at any selected spot, when the bow doors would open and men and equipment roll off as from a bridge and without any delay.

FORTRESS WALL OF EUROPE. The German nation had become very apprehensive about Allied invasion, and leading German speakers boasted that their fortifications and coast defenses on the coasts of the Atlantic and the Mediterranean were impregnable. Parties of press correspondents were conducted over these defenses, and returned to bolster up morale by repeating these boasts and assuring the German people that a successful invasion was impossible. Although their defenses were immensely strong,

the German claim that they could be equally strong along the whole coast line was ridiculous. These defenses included natural caverns on the coast, which the Germans had made invulnerable to bombing attacks from the air (left); gigantic guns in immensely strong positions (right); massed anti-tank obstacles, road blocks, entrenchments, and minefields. Huge bomb-proof shelters of steel and concrete were erected to house U-boats. Many of these positions were built by labor from the occupied countries.

Invasion of Italy steals the spotlight as fourth year ends

NEXT MEDITERRANEAN PHASE
British troops at Catania ready for
the invasion of the Italian mainland.

NOW THOSE WHO SOWED THE WIND
ARE REAPING THE WHIRLWIND

"There is no halting place at this
point. We have now reached a point
in the journey where there can be
no pause. We must go on."

Extract from Winston Churchill's speech
of September 6, 1943.